Between Sundays

Cover design and interior layout by Olivier Darbonville

ISBN 9798779712866

Between Sundays

Stories from childhood.
Lessons for life.

Nathan Thompson

with Katie Thompson

CONTENTS

MY SISTERS LOVINGLY REFER TO ME AS THE "GOLDEN CHILD," AND I HAVE SELFLESSLY CARRIED THIS BURDEN OF RESPONSIBILITY MY WHOLE LIFE.

Introduction

MANY PEOPLE WILL EXPERIENCE JESUS on Sunday at church, but what about the other six days of the week? What about what happens between Sundays? In my childhood home, God was central to our everyday life. He was present with us and involved in our journey. We didn't stop worshiping Jesus when we left church on Sunday, and following Him didn't take on a new form when the work week started Monday morning. Growing up in my home, we had the opportunity to see Jesus every day, and it was pretty amazing. To understand many of my stories, you'll need to become a little more familiar with the main players, my family.

My parents are from two different worlds. Mom grew up in Honduras in Central America, and Dad grew up in rural Michigan. They met in their twenties and were married within two weeks. As their love for one another grew, so did their love for Jesus.

I am the youngest of three kids. My oldest sister, Kara, was always more responsible than my middle sister, Cheryl, or me. She was easygoing, followed our mom and dad's rules, and was terrified of getting spankings. Parents all over the world are hoping and praying for children like her. Kara has always been loyal and sincere. She is direct but sensitive; I love that about her.

Then Cheryl came. Cheryl and Kara are about as different as a flower and a hand grenade. Cheryl came with a lot of sass, and she wasn't afraid of spankings. Sometimes I think she welcomed a fight like Neo from *The Matrix*. Cheryl has always been able to see value in people that can be easily overlooked or disregarded. She has a tender heart and compassion for the underdog.

My siblings are great, but Mom specifically prayed to God for me. After having two girls, Mom was ready for a boy. I am the youngest child, only son, and self-proclaimed favorite. My sisters lovingly refer to me as the "Golden Child," and I have selflessly carried this burden of responsibility my whole life.

The idea behind *Between Sundays* comes from my childhood experiences with my loving, fun, imperfect, God-loving family. I started a lecture series called Six Days of Jesus, where I spoke about six topics from

my childhood that made a lasting impact on my life. I presented the series at a local coffee shop and then repeated the lectures at my church. As I recounted the warm memories from childhood, it caused me to take stock of how I was leading my family. I had to ask myself, "Would my son have better stories than I did?" I felt compelled by God to be more conscious of my Monday through Saturday. Kate and I have been married for seventeen years at the time of this writing. Our son, Bear, is ten years old. As we explore living in faith, we have found ourselves using the topics in this book as a launching pad. Kate is the string to my balloon, the sea to my ship, and the gravity to my earth. I need her and enjoy every second of life with her. Bear was born to be great; the world needs him to be great, and God designed him to be great. I am encouraged every day by who he is becoming.

We have built upon the biblical foundation poured by my parents. Each of these topics was common in my home Monday through Saturday. We didn't follow Jesus flawlessly, but we did it consistently and as a family. These are stories from my life's experience. My hope is they become more than stories to you. I pray they inspire you to create your own stories with your Creator, to live Christianity between Sundays.

BONUS ROUNDS

I love a good story. But not every story I wanted to tell falls precisely in line with the book's key points. So, some stories didn't make the cut for the main text but couldn't be cut from the book altogether. As you read, you will stumble across these bonus episodes from my life. It'll be up to you to venture into the added nonsense, details, and perspectives these stories offer. They're peppered throughout the book so enjoying or bypassing them is up to you.

TALKING ABOUT
JESUS REGULARLY,
INVITING HIM
TO RECLINE AT
OUR TABLE, AND
HONORING HIS
SACRIFICE REMINDS
OUR FAMILY THAT WE
ARE PART OF GOD'S
GREAT PLAN FOR
HUMANITY.

CHAPTER ONE
Communion

W HAT DO YOU INSTANTLY IMAGINE WHEN you read the word "communion?" Where are you? Who is with you? How does communion look?

If you're like most people I know, you probably think of a communion ceremony at church. While my family did participate in church communion, for me, communion was primarily a family event when I was growing up.

The year was 1991. I was ten years old, sitting on the living room floor of my house, along with my two sisters and parents. We always gathered for communion around a worn-out coffee table. The furniture situation at home was something like a potluck you would have at work. There are always three people who bring chips and salsa and one who makes a Crockpot of meatballs. Another person makes buffalo chicken dip and sets it next to the two cheesy potatoes. Halfway through lunch, everyone is smiling at each other, giving courtesy compliments, "Oh wow, these

I am a registered nurse at a local hospital. Nurses love to eat at potlucks but hate having to remember to bring something. I brought a giant bag of corn chips and salsa once. The problem was my family had already started eating the chips earlier that week. So, I just acted like it was a new bag. I pretended to open the bag and started eating chips and salsa at 07:04 to throw my coworkers off my scent.

meatballs..." The food combination doesn't make sense, but potlucks always manage to work out, just like our furniture.

The coffee table had two open ends with a cabinet in the middle. The cabinet was a treasure trove of sewing magazines, greeting cards, and recipes acquired and preserved over the previous fifteen years. Mom was always just about to dig into these sassy boys, so donating them to Goodwill was out of the question.

I once crashed into this coffee table with my face and received a complimentary extraction of my two front teeth. I was about six years old, running full throttle through the length of our ranch-style home. Leaning over a yellow metal Tonka truck, I never let off the gas and lost control of the vehicle. My baby teeth were easily lost to the corner of the table. My mom was casually corded to the wall while using the old landline, chatting it up with my aunt. Panicked, I cupped my hand over my mouth. With blood and saliva flowing out of my tooth sockets, I ran to my mom. I tilted my hand down, and she could see the pool of blood and my two baby teeth dangling by their roots out of my mouth. We rushed to the

Sassy Boy (adjective) \'sa-se\ \'boi

Origin of phrase: my dad.

a: something neat that you or someone else owns

b: any sweet treat that will elevate your blood glucose levels

c: any object that may be trying to elude being eaten

Example: If a hotdog is rolling off the grill, you would yell to the chef, "Ope! grab that sassy boy!" If it falls to the deck, you would grab it and say, "Let me take care of this sassy boy." Then consume it with very, very little guilt and shame.

dentist, and he finished the job of dispatching my teeth. So, when we gathered for communion around this table, I remembered both the blood I shed from my Tonka truck crash and the blood Jesus shed for me.

My parents were consistent in initiating communion as a family. They took the Scripture from Isaiah 53:5 very seriously, "...by his wounds we are healed" (New International Version). Any ailment would prompt the preparation of the communion table. If our cousins (who were our best friends and neighbors) were all sick with diarrhea and vomiting, my sisters and I knew we would be taking communion soon. Like the sound of a tornado siren going off in the distance, we would hear our parents' voices blaring through the house, "The Vincents are sick; we are having communion tonight," as they battened down the hatches and got out the juice and bread.

We received the elements as we prayed for health and thanked Jesus for the stripes He took for us. Receiving His body and blood was a better first line of defense than going to the doctor. But my parents didn't need a specific reason to take communion. They sincerely desired that we remember Jesus' death and resurrection as a family, so we took communion often.

In my young mind, the elements were essential to having a successful communion. When we bought juice, I always wanted 100% Welch's grape juice. One time Cheryl picked out white grape juice because she thought it would be cool. I knew that communion wouldn't count because of the inferior juice my sinful sister chose. It was like that scene in *Indiana Jones and the Last Crusade* where he had to choose the right cup at the end of the movie. My sister was too fancy, too showy, too careless in her drink choice. She "chose poorly." Everyone who loves the Lord knows He desires 100% Welch's *red* grape juice at the table. I can also remember using orange juice from concentrate and cranberry juice when options were limited.

On another occasion, Kara thought we should share the cup as the disciples did. We did it. It was disgusting. By the time the cup got to me, it was one part His blood and four parts their saliva. Our shared cup had practically become communion bread pudding for the last one to partake. Our home experience with the practice of communion was different from our experience at church. It was messy, loud, and awkward at times, but it was real and powerful.

Taking communion as a family taught me three simple things:

First, we don't need a mediator between God and us.

Second, we are the church; we don't go to church.

Third, remembering Jesus resets our compass.

Let's use the following passage from Luke to examine these three points:

> *Dad: "We're having communion; mix this." He hands me a frozen can of orange juice concentrate.*
>
> *Me: Mumbling under my breath, "Well, this one won't count."*
>
> *Me: Twenty minutes later, after thawing our juice, "Ready!"*
>
> *Family: Disappointedly stares at a two-inch cube of orange juice concentrate bobbing in the pitcher as Dad reads the holy Scripture.*
>
> *Me: Not listening to anything Dad is saying, just thinking, "Sorry Lord, next time we will have 100% Welch's; forgive us."*

When the hour came, Jesus and his apostles reclined at the table. And he said to them, "I have eagerly desired to eat this Passover with you before I suffer. For I tell you, I will not eat it again until it finds fulfillment in the kingdom of God."

After taking the cup, he gave thanks and said, "Take this and divide it among you. For I tell you I will not drink again from the fruit of the vine until the kingdom of God comes."

And he took bread, gave thanks and broke it, and gave it to them, saying, "This is my body given for you; do this in remembrance of me." In the same way, after the supper he took the cup, saying, "This cup is the new covenant in my blood, which is poured out for you." (Luke 22:14-20 NIV)

We don't need a mediator between God and us.

Do you find it challenging to have a one-on-One relationship with God?

The passage in Luke sets the scene with Jesus and His disciples about to take communion. Reading in Luke "Jesus and his disciples reclined at the table", we see that the setting was comfortable and casual. Our family's communion setting paralleled this. I remember my dad sitting on the floor leaning against the couch in his white V-neck Hanes t-shirt with one arm spread over the cushions. He would read the communion story from his torn-up *Dake Study Bible* with chicken scratch notes in the margins. My memories of my dad as a kid have created him to be a man's man in my adult mind. He was strong. He was steady. He could do anything.

Dad worked as a machinist at NAPA Auto Parts Store for most of my childhood. His hands were the hands of a mechanic, grease in all the tiny creases of his knuckles. Oil that seemed never to wash away. If something broke around the house, he'd fix it. We never called a repairman because Dad would handle it. (I am now the proud owner of my childhood home, and I wonder if maybe we should've called a maintenance specialist a time or two.) I recall sitting on my dad's lap when he would get home from work. I would take his wedding ring off his hand and put it on mine. I would put my hand in his. His hand was

the size of a catcher's mitt. As our family all sat on the floor around the little coffee table for communion, my dad would be right down on the floor with us, reclined at the table.

Jesus kept this sacred moment with His disciples both casual and personal. There was no room for religious order because religion would make it awkward. This moment was between friends. This moment was with family. 1 Timothy 2:5 reminds us, "there is one God and one mediator between God and mankind, the man Christ Jesus" (NIV). The mediator to God is God. To truly commune with Him is to invite Him to the table of our life and recline there with Him.

Communion at my place of worship is beautiful. Together in unity, music in the background, our pastor guides us in remembering what God did to adopt us into His family. Receiving communion with others is essential. However, when I receive communion only at church, the moment can feel more like a toast at a wedding than a personal connection as a bride has with her groom. During a toast, the speaker honors the person being celebrated. The guests' attention is divided between the guest of honor and the speaker.

In some ways, communion taken only as ritual or tradition with someone else's presence required is like a toast, showing devotion and remembrance, but losing the intimacy of its original design. The person toasting becomes a mediator between the attendees and, in the case of a wedding, the groom. Guests' eyes are often drawn back and forth between the two. I have to ask, how personal do you want communion to be? To me, it should be face-to-face with the Groom Himself.

While communion at church is a huge part of worship, the communion I took at home with my tribe changed my life. When Christ himself approached communion, He lay back on some pillows with His friends. Referring to the Scriptures in Luke, we see that the disciples were eye to eye with the Savior. No one mediating between them and Christ. Direct connection. In the same way, we don't need a priest or bishop or pastor to lead us. We simply need to prepare the table, lean back, and be with God.

The dictionary defines communion as the sharing or exchanging of intimate thoughts and feelings. Can you have true intimacy with someone when a middleman is required to get you there? Institutions and people should not be established mediators in my relationship with God. I understand that as Christ's body we share in communion, and we should, but unlike a toast at a wedding, our eyes should always be captivated with the Groom, not the best man.

> The best man's speech at my wedding was a debacle. The D.J. said in the mic, "Let's make a toast," and handed the mic to my best man. Mark nervously said who-knows-what and raised a glass. The problem was, I had an empty glass, so my expert D.J. poured his drink into my glass and laughed. I just stared at him and took a sip. That guy was a meatball.

My life is the table I prepare and give to commune with
God. Sunday is a place to start, but it's not enough. Most of
what I do on Sunday is listening and learning, but one day
doesn't provide a full opportunity to live what I've learned. I
am missing the point if I only come to Christ on a Sunday
when I receive something. If there is no exchange of life with
Him between Sundays, I will lose the closeness because I need
someone else to connect me.

We don't go to church; we are the church.

Is your relationship with God dependent on a building?

At one time, my local church started renting a space to
hold our Sunday morning service. The part I liked most about
our situation was that the building wasn't ours. We had to
share it with the community. We had to "bring" the church
every time we went on Sundays. Monday through Saturday,
concerts, plays, and ceremonies would take place in the au-
ditorium. Props and stage sets often remained set up for the
Sunday matinee. The set of *Mama Mia* was fun, the *Lion King*
and *Willy Wonka* were fascinating, but *The Rocky Horror Picture Show* was my favorite because it came with a catwalk.
What worship leader doesn't want a catwalk for Christ? On
Sunday morning, we showed up, set up, and prepared to enter
the presence of God. The building was not the church. The
people were the church.

This point came up when hosting the Six Days of Jesus
lecture series in early 2019. I asked: how would our relationship with God change without church? Then, it happened.
During the COVID-19 pandemic, many churches closed for

a time or went online. Did this change your relationship with God? The realization that "we don't go to church, we are the church" was forced into the spotlight and examined. I felt like I'd been riding a tandem bike for years, and now, my spiritual life was wobbling on a unicycle. It was time to ride or die. Thankfully, I had a little practice leading my siblings in small, terrible church services as a kid at home.

Despite church "how-we-knew-it" changing, Kate and I started an Instagram Bible study through the book of James. We held three micro-conferences. We started a Bible study in our house that lasted a year and a half going through John, Acts, and Romans. We created opportunities for people to meet Jesus instead of waiting for "normal."

When we had communion as a family, my dad would have the kids take turns leading. On my turn, I'm sure I'd have a nervous half-grin, trading glances with my sisters as we butchered traditional communion. I remember the part where we would have to "search our heart." First, I would tell everyone to pray for God to reveal any sin in their life. Then, I would scan the room to see who stopped praying first. If one of my sisters were the first to finish their introspection, I would raise my eyebrows, thinking, "yeah, right… keep searching, sinner. There's no way you're done." Then, I can remember wondering if I missed anything in myself.

A particular Scripture about communion caused me a lot of anxiety. We read in 1 Corinthians 11:27-29:

> So then, whoever eats the bread or drinks the cup of the LORD in an unworthy manner will be guilty of sinning against the body and blood of the LORD. Everyone

ought to examine themselves before they eat of the bread and drink from the cup. For those who eat and drink without discerning the body of Christ eat and drink judgment on themselves. (NIV)

Specifically, the words "examine themselves" concerned me. I didn't want to be one of the judged or cursed ones the Bible talks about. I was nervous that I didn't examine deeply enough, and I'd drink God's judgment on myself. I was worried that I wasn't worthy, and there was a death sentence looming just around the corner. Have you ever associated this same sense of guilt with taking communion? I thought I was supposed to search for every sin I'd committed, confess, and repent so I could be worthy and *then* approach God. What if I forgot to ask for forgiveness for when I lost my temper, lied to my parents, or disrespected my teachers? It seemed impossible to examine enough. Re-read verse 29, "For those who eat and drink without discerning the body of Christ eat and drink judgment on themselves." To discern, by definition, is to perceive or recognize. We aren't asked to acknowledge *our* bodies but to recognize *His*.

Judgment comes when we don't discern Him. The examination isn't of our sins but His righteousness. When we feel unworthiness during communion, experienced as judgment, guilt, or condemnation, we

> Mom and Dad always took the longest to "search their hearts." I thought they were super close to God, but now that I have a child, I realize what was happening. They had way more problems they were working through than us kids. Three of their biggest challengers were sitting next to them around the coffee table, fighting with each other.

take our eyes off the Groom and put our focus back on ourselves. When I scrutinize all I have done wrong, I feel judged. But when I discern the body of Christ, I find freedom. We need to examine our perception and recognition of Christ. We don't need to get ourselves right before we approach God. If we recognize that Jesus is the Righteous One, we are worthy and accepted.

When my parents taught me how to lead communion, I learned how to speak directly to God for myself. I knew that, in Him, I was worthy to talk to God. This life lesson allowed the church to become an additional resource to commune with God rather than my only resource. Leading communion was more than learning to pray. It was weightier than a prayer. We didn't make requests during communion, and it wasn't about me getting something. Instead, it was about me thanking someone. I recognized who Jesus is and chose to discern His body rather than dwell on my sins or imperfections.

I also learned that Jesus looks forward to being with me. In Luke 22:15, Jesus says, "'I have eagerly desired to eat this Passover with you.'" There I was in my pajamas, sitting on the floor with grape juice and saltines, remembering the suf-

> Jesus tells us to renew our minds daily. He tells us as often as we eat, remember Him through communion. Recognizing His broken body reminds us that His nature can be our nature, that His mind can be ours. We can have the mind of Christ. When I have my wife's mind, I can access her perspectives, beliefs, and reasoning. Who wouldn't want to have the mind of Christ, access to His knowledge, wisdom, and attitudes? Communion can be a fresh way to renew your mind.

fering and death of God with my family. After we had taken communion together, my mom and dad would often end by saying, "We love doing this with you guys. We've been looking forward to this time. We have been eagerly waiting to be with you in this all week." And Jesus says, "'I have eagerly desired to eat this with you.'" With you. Not with a building, not with a denomination, not with a religious practice, but with you.

Communion resets our compass.

How often have you thought, "I should have communion to remember Christ outside of church?"

Throughout life, we often reflect on testimonies of what God brought us out of and what we would be like without Him. In other words, we reflect on the benefits of what Christ has done. But communion is a bit different. Communion is the ultimate reminder of who Christ is, not the benefits to us of what He has done. We read Jesus' words, "After taking the cup, he gave thanks and said, 'Take this and divide it among you. For I tell you I will not drink again from the fruit of the vine until the kingdom of God comes.' And he took bread, gave thanks and broke it, and gave it to them, saying, 'This is my body given for you; do this in remembrance of me.'" (Luke 22:17-19 NIV). Communion is the purest form of strictly remembering the blood of the Lamb. I believe this because we aren't the source of the blood, but we are the benefactors of it.

Stopping to remember Jesus through communion reminds us that we love Him because He first loved us (1 John 4:19 New King James Version); not that we love Him for what we see He brought us out of. Communion says, "Thank You for what You did." That's it. Not, "Thank You for what You did for me." We do not hold a part in this section of the story. It has all to do with Him. Only Him. We come before Him to look into His eyes and say thank you.

In addition, communion reconfigures what we view as important. We often believe we know what is most important, and it isn't easy to see it any other way. For example, I work as a nurse in the Cardiovascular Lab at our local hospital. During my weekend on call, if someone has an emergency, like a heart attack, I book-it to the hospital. The hospital called me in one Saturday afternoon, and God showed me a new view of importance. The car in front of me was taking their sweet time driving down the road, and I thought, "If this person's loved one was having a heart attack, they would be moving a lot faster to let me get to the hospital." God spoke to my heart, and my mind followed Him down this path.

It would be impossible for me to convince someone whose loved one had a heart attack that it was more critical for me to be at the hospital than them. It would be absurd to the person for me to say, "You don't even need to be at the hospital if I'm there." The only way it wouldn't be ridiculous would be if they knew I'd be helping to fix the problem. Sometimes, we believe we know what is most valuable in life, but maybe we've gotten ahead of the most important thing. Maybe we've been driving along, assuming we know what's best for us and what's best for us is in the car behind us. But there are moments we need to slow down and get a new vantage point.

Communion with Jesus reminds us of what's most significant, taking us off autopilot to look for Him. Seeing Him adjusts our perspective and broadens our scope. Our worries and problems become overshadowed by gratitude for what He's done. When we acknowledge Jesus, we don't look around at our life circumstances; we look at Him.

Communion will not only realign you with J.C., but it'll also bring your family closer together. Talking about Jesus regularly, inviting Him to recline at our table, and honoring His sacrifice reminds our family that we are part of God's great plan for humanity. Jesus is the family's core, and communion reminds us of His presence in our lives.

We have the opportunity to take communion daily. Jesus made this very simple for us. And when we receive it, we are reminded that we now live in His nature. His broken body shattered human nature. Think about that. Man has been forging a new way since the fall of Adam, using selfish motives and ambitions to accomplish this new path. A path to nowhere. A self-created, self-centered nature that continually leads us away from God. Jesus said, "'My body was broken for you'" (Luke 22:19 NIV). He broke the back of human nature so we could take on His character and heart. The nature of the Father. The fruit of His Spirit. That is who we are now.

We are whole, in health, soul, mind, and strength because that is what the nature of God is (Romans Chapter 6). Total restoration. We can now renew our minds daily (Romans 12:2) with communion. The blood seals this in us. It is the blood of the new covenant, a covenant that says you have been restored and made brand new (2 Corinthians 5:17).

I encourage you to take time to do communion at home. It may be uncomfortable if you haven't done it before. But in reality, it's not awkward; it's just new. Someone may spill the juice. You may forget what Scriptures to read. Or your Spotify worship playlist may start a commercial about air fresheners right when you begin "examining your heart." How something starts doesn't define how it finishes. It will be powerful and beautiful.

Recounting the origins of communion in my life is special to me, but, more importantly, bringing my family into this practice has started a legacy of remembering our Savior. For a few years now, my wife Kate and I have been putting this into practice with our son, Bear. The first time we did, it took about two minutes. It was uncomfortable, kind of funny, but one hundred percent authentic. It was like my family had a private meeting with God. Now, Bear likes to read the Scriptures and prepare the juice and bread (or water and crackers if that's all we have). Any one of us will initiate having communion together, and it wouldn't be unusual to have communion individually. It's simple, but deep.

My parents genuinely led us how Christ led the disciples. As you continue reading the chapter in Luke, a dispute broke out among the disciples immediately following communion. They started arguing about who was the best, which is what my sisters and I usually did. Remember, if there wasn't a fight, it wasn't right! Now go for it.

WHEN WE'VE
MADE OURSELVES
VULNERABLE, SET
ASIDE INSECURITIES
AND COMPARISON, AND
MADE TIME TO GROW
WITH EACH OTHER,
WE HAVE NOURISHED
BEAUTIFUL
FRIENDSHIPS THAT
WILL STAND THE TEST
OF TIME AND THE TEST
OF AWKWARD BIBLE
STUDIES.

CHAPTER TWO
Bible Study

Community- A feeling of fellowship with others, as a result of sharing common attitudes, interests, and goals.

M Y PARENTS HAD VARIOUS WAYS OF CREATING community and studying the Bible. One, in particular, was going to my aunt's house. My parents, aunts, and uncles would read the Bible and sometimes sing worship songs together in my aunt's basement. I can see them sprinkled around the room, some singing louder than others, a few standing, and others sitting—all of them pursuing connection with God and each other. My mom had her tambourine, my aunt played the keyboard, and my uncle played guitar. All the kids played outside while the grown-ups did their thing. We had a big extended family with lots of cousins, so kids were always around to play.

Another time I remember going to a couple's house from church for a Bible study. This experience was a little different from being at my aunt's house. The couple had a quaint place in the city, so space was limited. The

I know this isn't what I saw, but it's how the memory wants to feel. Mom swaying back and forth with her tambourine, silk scarves everywhere, a brown flower print blouse, six different scents of incense burning, Dad nodding to the beat, tight white deep V-neck (obviously), all my aunts and uncles on a magic carpet ride with Jesus. Basically "The Doors" jam session without the shrooms.

parents would all pack into the living room, and they crammed us kids in the bedroom. I'm sure the fire marshal would have said it was a violation and shut that book club down. It had the same feeling as when you see those news stories of people housing twenty to thirty stray dogs in a back bedroom of their house. All the kids hoped for fresh air and a snack while our parents laughed and read the Holy scriptures. It was like they never once read where Jesus said, "let the little children come unto me." When we would go into the adult room, we'd promptly get yelled at to play somewhere else. But there wasn't anywhere else. They were in the "somewhere else" we wanted to be.

In addition to going other places, my parents often had Bible study in our own home, around that same worn-out coffee table. Real-life situations happened when my parents had people over to our house for Bible study. We had a wiener dog named Oscar. Oscar thought he was the alpha male of the house and liked to show it. One night at the Bible study, that bold little hot dog dragged his toy companion out into the middle of the room and started to establish dominance over the innocent stuffed bear. He was showing off for all our spiritual friends. My mom and her

There I was, wishing I wasn't in that sweatshop of a house with eight other prepubescent and pubescent kids without deodorant. Then, finally, one of the adult humans came into the prison yard they called a bedroom and had a box of bomb pops, handed them out, then disappeared like a Seal Team Six soldier. I then went to the kitchen to toss out the wrapper and popsicle stick and caught an earful from the same philanthropist who'd handed out life-giving popsicles—slapped by the hand that fed me.

friend, Lucy, shouted to interrupt Oscar's passion. Dad was cracking up, and I just stared with an awkward smile on my face in complete disbelief. Mom, Dad, and their church guests paused discussion on the goodness of God while Oscar had his own spiritual experience.

It's fun to relive these memories because Kate and I have now experienced similar situations as adults. Years ago, Kate had a women's group that met at our house, and one of the little girls came into the living room and calmly said, "Bear needs your help." So, she went to see what our little fella needed and found there was poop peppered everywhere. In the bathroom, the hallway, his bedroom. He was potty training. In one fell swoop, she put Bear in the bathtub and shooed the other children out of the contaminated areas. Then, with a rush in her step and Lysol wipes in her hand, she did her best to clean it up. Returning to her guests, she apologized for the interruption and hoped no one would catch a sniff of poop mixed with Fresh Linen Febreze billowing down the hallway.

We have hosted Bible study groups as a family and are here to report that some things never change. Weird stuff happens, humbling stuff happens, and real-life happens. But building relationships with God and each other through Bible study is worth every effort. What it showed me was that living in community is part of God's design.

> Bible study has taught me three main things:
> First, engaging with others is encouraging.
> Second, it's challenging to be open.
> And third, it's best to grow with friends.

Scripture shows how the early church lived in community:

> They devoted themselves to the apostles' teaching and to fellowship, to the breaking of bread and to prayer. Everyone was filled with awe at the many wonders and signs performed by the apostles. All the believers were together and had everything in common. They sold property and possessions to give to anyone who had need. Every day they continued to meet together in the temple courts. They broke bread in their homes and ate together with glad and sincere hearts, praising God and enjoying the favor of all the people. And the Lord added to their number daily those who were being saved. (Acts 2:42-47 NIV)

Let's set the scene: it was an early fall evening in lower Michigan. Perfect 62 degrees with a light breeze. The sun was setting behind the trees. The kids and Golden-doodles were frolicking around the yard, and our friends gathered around a smokeless fire. My wife was reading through Romans chapter seven as I was sipping my coffee while surrounded by friends. F.B.S., Friends Bible Study, in its glory. All of a sudden, I launched to my feet as though someone deployed an airbag under my chair and began to scream in my best dad voice, "Bear! Quit pushing him!" I stormed out of the fellowship circle toward the scene of said incident. I lay into all the kids about pushing and wrestling on the treehouse. Then, like a Jekyll and Hyde scenario, I calmly walked back to the circle, so chill as if nothing ever happened. I gently asked Kate, "Read that last part again?" Everyone, including myself, was like, "What the heck just happened?"

Then, my neighbor kid stopped over and yelled, "Hi Nate," and proceeded to join the chaos of kids. At some point, he took off his shirt and magically transformed into a human dinosaur that roared impressively loud with a tone, pitch, and accuracy that no human child should be able to attain. This set all the designer dogs on red alert. The dogs squared up like Blue, Delta, and Charlie from Jurassic World at the scene when that kid falls in the cage. They were ready to eat; it was a surreal experience. The moral of the story is sometimes Bible Study Night escalates, and you have to be prepared at any moment to jump in the cage, like Chris Pratt, to keep people from dying.

Engaging with others is encouraging.

How often is it a challenge for you to engage with people?

Let's start with verse 44, "All the believers were together and had everything in common." That sounds impossible to me. Just think about that sentence: They had everything in common. I don't believe the Scripture is talking about liking the same ice cream or t-shirt or cars. I don't think this means they rooted for the same sports team or shared hobbies, careers, or social interests. I do believe this means they engaged in each other's lives. They shared the same goal, the same vision, the same dream. Jesus. He is the "everything in common."

The early disciples were coming together often. They were living life together and sharing their outcomes of both victories and failures so that they could be effective in their corporate goal. They were starting to understand their identity and were functioning as the church. The believers lived individual lives but were completely connected through their common purpose.

This idea brings me back to being a kid in school. Thirty kids were given the same image to color, and they all turned out completely different yet the same. In kindergarten each week, we had a caricature of a letter of the alphabet to color. I can recall coloring Mr. H. He had wild green hair. The picture itself gave us kids all things in common. Mr. H was our outline and mission. We personalized Mr. H according to creative preferences and skill level. When my classmates and I finished, I saw pictures that were different than mine.

At this point, I could glean for the purpose of learning or compare to see where I stacked up. Something that kills the vulnerable, innocence of teachability is comparison. The endpoint of comparing similar things is to judge which one is better. Instead of appreciating variety, we can devalue ourselves or others.

As I grew and became "wiser" and "smarter," learning turned into a way of sizing myself up. Like the kids coloring pictures, I'd twist the idea of gleaning knowledge from someone into, "You think you're better than me," or "I'll never be as good as you." We put people in categories and label them to understand how we stack up. We want to hide the parts of us that we feel aren't good enough and elevate our areas of excellence. But this process limits our growth, promotes pride over humility, and diminishes the ability to be honest and exposed. Comparison kills vulnerability. It leads to disengagement, which is the enemy of community. I'm certain the disciples had differences, but they never lost sight of the outline they had in common.

We all have something to offer, and we all have something to learn. When my parents were new believers at their Bible study, they brought a new set of eyes, teachability, and a fresh perspective. At the same time, they gained knowledge, background, and deeper understanding from others. They grew together by displaying humility and rejecting rivalry.

A Scripture from Proverbs shows how we can help each other grow. Proverbs 27:17 says, "As iron sharpens iron, so one person sharpens another" (NIV). This wise Proverb brings a sense of camaraderie needed in our circle of friends and family. We can be proud of our differences and use them to help one another. In contrast, comparison wants to separate and seclude us. We also need to remember that our strengths don't make us better than or less than others.

I can see the perceived tiers of value that come with comparison in my workplace. A nurse aide may feel less than a nurse because they easily compare their knowledge or skillset in the healthcare setting. I can see the other nurses looking in the face of a doctor with a sense of fear that they'll say something wrong and be embarrassed or make a mistake and be ashamed. And I've seen doctors, who are very good at their craft, belittle others for not having knowledge that is second nature to them. This dynamic creates a potential pecking order in the hospital that can make people feel less than someone else. But one day, God gave me another perspective.

One of the physicians I work with asked me to come to his house to do some handy work. The things I did seemed so simple to me, so I told him I couldn't charge him. I fixed a couple of cupboard handles, tightened some screws, and replaced some boards on a deck. He was amazed at my ability to fix things, while I was amazed at his ability to help people with their health. I left his house and thought about how we really are all equal. We have various skill sets and interests, but that shouldn't affect how we view our God-given value as people. If we feel less than someone else, it limits our ability to have authentic, engaging conversations.

You see, engaging with people is vulnerable. And going into relationships with insecurities and false securities creates an environment in our minds that wants to compare. We walk into a room as fully grown, successful people but are uncomfortable in our skin. We take what we view as shortcomings and compare them to fake, made-up expectations of what other people think about us. I suspect the majority of the time, the other people around us aren't even thinking what we think they're thinking. That's because most other people are doing the same thing.

This dangerous cycle stunts our growth and the development of our community. Instead, we should value who we are and appreciate what we have to offer. The early church supported each other by being involved in each other's lives. We need to live in a place where we can celebrate someone's successes and genuinely help others through failures.

The believers also encouraged one another through their individual and collective growth in God. The Scripture in Acts says, "They sold property and possessions to give to anyone in need." In addition, in the New Testament we read, "Therefore encourage one another and build each other up, just as in fact you are doing" (1 Thessalonians 5:11 NIV). To sell a property and give away possessions, you must know God personally and be encouraged by people who think like Him.

Have you ever been around someone whose presence and language cause you to be inspired? Not jealous, not dis-

When I heard Craig was coming with all the soaps and fancy lotions, I thought I would return the favor and grill him a delicious steak. The problem was I didn't know how to cook a steak and had no concept of what a good cut of meat was. So, I went to the tiny local grocery store and bought a half-inch thick steak for $8. For all I knew, it could have been a pork chop. I grilled hamburgers for everyone else and made the steak for Craig. While trying to cook that sassy boy, the grill ran out of propane, but I powered through. Craig graciously offered to eat a hamburger, but I insisted this steak was what he truly wanted. So, I went inside to finish my Mona Lisa off in a frying pan. I'm sure it was the grossest thing he had eaten since college, but Craig didn't complain.

couraged, but inspired. I met a man in Pennsylvania when I was in a band. His name was Craig. Craig was like no one I had ever met. He used language in a way I had never heard. He said things like "connect heart to heart," "Sometimes my schedule's crazy, but I like it that way," and my favorite, "Let's get a little custard action." Craig and his wife had beautiful hearts and were very generous and caring.

Too many times to count, Craig treated us like we were already on VH1's, *Where Are They Now?* He was great. He put us up in Hiltons around the country on countless occasions so we didn't have to sleep in our van. He also brought a pallet of different household items to my house to divide up with my bandmates to help us out. Craig made me want to be a better

This story sums up the spirit of Craig's friendship. He called me and asked how the band was doing and how the guys were all holding up. "Great," I said, "We are on our way to our next show." When he asked where we were sleeping for the night, I told him we'd sleep in the van or somewhere cheap. Craig said he'd take care of it and put us up in a Hilton that was on the way to our next show.

He called me back and said we were all set; the front desk would be looking for us when we arrived. When we pulled in, two workers held goody bags with cookies and water and offered to take our luggage. They let us swim in the pool and hot tub even though it was after 2 a.m. They were intrigued about the band and honored us like royalty. Come to find out, Craig made us sound like one of the biggest bands in the Christian Rock genre. We weren't. What they didn't know was we had been wearing the same clothes for days because they were the coolest outfits we had. We planned to wash our shirts that night in the sink—perception is 9/10s of band law.

person, to be a "Craig" to others I would meet along the way.

When we intentionally engage in life with friends, it propels us to be our best.

Connecting with others should be a priority in everyone's life. At times I've done the opposite. Not only have I erected a privacy fence in the backyard of my home, but I've also put one in the backyard of my mind. Will you be honest and admit you have to? We block people out or don't let them in. We ghost friends and foes out of convenience to our daily objectives. It feels exhausting to lift our brains over the top of the privacy fence to talk to an acquaintance at the grocery store. Instead, we stare at the ingredients on the bag of potatoes, hoping our neighbor will ignore us too and keep moseying toward the yogurt section.

Everyone has reasons for being guarded or reclusive. Some have struggled through rejection time after time. Some of us have insecurities holding us back. Others have been wearing a mask for so long, they can't imagine someone seeing who they are below the surface. Countless other (very understandable) reasons exist for disconnecting. But if we want fruitful lives in our homes, at work, in our churches, and our community, we've got to take a step forward to interact with each other in meaningful ways.

We all have resources to gain and give when we live in community as the disciples did. Every day we can choose encouragement over comparison and remind ourselves we have all things in common.

Is it hard for you to be open with people?

Living in a close community with others means we will be cultivating sincere relationships. We will celebrate with each other in victory and work through difficult seasons. We will exchange stories and look for advice.

At times, conversations will be uncomfortable. But the short-term discomfort can lead to long-term growth. The Bible talks about a closeness in relationships that involves looking into someone's eyes and exchanging truth. To live in close fellowship, we need to be open to correction and helping others when something is off.

Jesus spoke to this in Luke 6:41-42: "And why worry about a speck in your friend's eye when you have a log in your own? How can you think of saying, 'Friend, let me help you get rid of that speck in your eye,' when you can't see past the log in your own eye? Hypocrite! First get rid of the log in your own eye; then you will see well enough to deal with the speck in your friend's eye'" (New Living Translation).

Most of the time, I read this Scripture and think, "I better not judge anyone because I don't want to be a hypocritical jerk like this guy." Or "I don't want to seem holier than my friend, so it's better not to say anything at all." But I believe this example goes further. The goal isn't to "not judge" and ignore the specks and planks. Instead, we should be brave enough to help one another with the sin, problems, or issues affecting our vision.

The issue was not that this guy was a jerk and always judged people. He had friends; Jesus said it. He said when you get the plank out of your eye, you can help your friend. So, the opposite must be true here. We must be willing to let a friend remove planks from our eyes. When a friend points to something in our life that needs correction, listen instead of being offended. The problem with the man in Luke was that he was not open with his friends about his issues, questions, or struggles. He only wanted to be available to fix theirs. That's what made him a hypocrite.

We need to be willing to entrust our friends with the vision and view of events in our life that cause specks to fall in our eyes. To be willing to ask them to help us remove obstacles that blind us from seeing clearly. If we have invested in close companions, they may see something that has become so close to us, we identify with it and don't even view it as a problem anymore. Removing a plank from our eyes can be painful and humbling. But the vulnerability it produces will often bring us closer to the people around us.

We act like people shouldn't invade our spiritual space, but Jesus says at the end of verse 42, "then you will see well enough to deal with the speck in your friend's eye." You have to be right up in someone's business to get something out of their eye. The hypocrisy is found in the one-sided vulnerability. You are a hypocrite if you are a friend that's not being open, honest, and vulnerable to the people in your crew. But, if you let a friend get a plank out of your eye, they'll trust you more to help them with the speck in theirs.

To have this level of trust in relationships means we need to be willing to go deeper with the people in our lives. We often allow people to see the surface of our emotions, but we don't go deep enough to ask for advice, correction, or guidance. Instead, we comment on our current state of mind on social media and wait for a flood of responses. If someone responds with intention, in a way that requires us to get eyes on our motives, we may become frustrated and disregard their concern. When we have hurt and pain in our life, we look for it in others, whether to find comfort or justification. We would rather have a superficial like on Meta (Facebook) or press of the heart button on our Instagram than genuine concern. Being open to feedback in the middle of our mess can feel painful. But not being receptive to guidance and sorting through life with a plank in our eye is dangerous.

> My Enneagram test results told me I was an Eight, nicknamed The Challenger. Initially, the Eight sounded like a real jerk. Convinced the test was wrong, I retook it—same result. I told Kate what happened, and her response was, "You're challenging the test. It labeled you a Challenger, and you disagree. Sounds accurate." I then realized Eights aren't jerks; they're questioning leads to progress.

At times, I've been proactive in sorting through my planks. I have had a general interest in personality types for years. It has always been intriguing to staple someone down with a letter, number, or animal that quickly describes them. The latest and greatest one I've used is the Enneagram. I am an Enneagram 8, a Challenger, on this test. It seems pretty accurate.

My friend, Scott, digs personality types too. He sent me a podcast in which a fellow "Challenger" was interviewed. At the end, he said, "Every Enneagram 8 person should ask someone they trust this question: What do you know about me, that I don't know about me, that I should know about me?" (Cron). When he said that, I was instantly secretly excited to hear someone answer this. I have a weirdness in me that enjoys raw feedback. The unhealthy part of me likes to use it as a starting point to pick a fight, but the healthy side craves the insight to improve how people experience me.

So, I reached out to Scott to answer the question and told him he had to say the answer to my face. He declined initially as a good introvert would, but I squeezed my body into that little safe place he tried to withdraw to and convinced him I needed him to do this for me. I trusted Scott to show me something I couldn't see for myself. He had every opportunity to poke me in the eye, but instead, he was thoughtful and helpful in showing me a speck that clouded my vision. Scott then returned the favor, asking the question back to me.

There we were, like a couple of monkeys on a tree branch. We were combing through each other's back hair for the fleas and ticks of life, making each other look good. But you can only go so deep into healing, correction,

I was working in the Electrophysiology Lab, and one of my coworkers randomly started blinking spastically and picking at his eyelid. His contact migrated to the back of his eyeball, and he was getting frantic while I made fun of him in disbelief. It finally shifted from funny to sad when he couldn't resolve the situation. I said, "Matt, you're gonna have to trust me." I went and grabbed a 0.9 flush syringe and had Matt sit in a chair with his head tilted back. I squirted the fluid into his eye, hoping I wasn't about to flush a contact lens deeper into his brain. Thank God it worked. The contact floated to the front of his eyeball. He plucked it out, rinsed it, and reinserted it. Sometimes you have to let someone help, even if it's outside their scope of practice.

and understanding with a friend. There's a point where we need to take what they've said to the Father and verify what's true. Clarity comes through one-on-One time with God. He wants to hear who we think we are so He can remind us who He created us to be. He wants to know us.

The same one-sided vulnerability showing itself in relationships with people can appear in our relationship with God. We learn about Him through the Bible, books, podcasts, and church. He makes Himself available to us. Through Jesus, we have direct access to Him. Through the Holy Spirit, we have His counsel and comfort. But do we let Him know our heart? Jesus's words in Matthew 7:22-23 are challenging: "'Many will say to me on that day, 'LORD, LORD, did we not prophesy in your name and in your name drive out demons and in your name perform many miracles?' Then I will tell them plainly, "I never knew you. Away from me, you evildoers!"'" (NIV). These verses are a reminder to invite into

I'll share Scott's response. I had him text it to me after he said it so I wouldn't change words in my mind to alter the meaning.

Jan 11, 2019

I feel you jump in with both feet, but you get burnt out or maybe bored and move on to the next thing. I feel you're searching for relevance, and that you're so eager to see the tangible fruits of your impact. God wants you to know that you won't see the majority of your impact. Like ripples, you can't see how far they reach. You won't fully realize the level of your impact until you reach Heaven. It may be the 8 (challenger) in you to want to change your world. Just don't get discouraged when you don't see right away the tangible fruits of your impact. Sometimes when we don't see it, we downplay our influence or impact. Be encouraged! 😊😬

our lives a heart-to-heart relationship with Christ. Do we allow Him to search the intimate parts of us that have experienced both satisfaction and disappointment? Are we open to His perfect guidance and correction? If God is at the center of our community, being honest with Him will have a gentle, organic ripple effect on the rest of our lives.

Let's accept the challenge. Let's be open with God and our community. Taking action to open our hearts will fan the flames that burn the planks. The ashes left become the fertilizer for our future growth with others.

It's best to grow with others in community.

Do you have a community of people who inspire you and challenge you?

We are designed to foster friendships and have companions, and who we choose as friends matters. We read in Proverbs 13:20, "Walk with the wise and become wise, for a companion of fools suffers harm" (NIV). Having a group of people chasing the same thing can help bring out our fullest potential. For example, runners who run alone may never push their limits. But having a group to run with encourages us to run harder and faster, find a sustainable pace in the stretches of life that require it, and finish strong. Even if we're not running the same track, we can drive one another forward if we have all things in common. However, if we're becoming jealous, bitter, or insecure with our friends, we need to resolve the root problem. Jealousy and bitterness often result from seeing someone's success in an area where we are struggling. We might feel insecure when we are around someone doing what they were meant to do when we aren't doing what we're meant to do.

I've been there. It's a terrible place to live. It's a self-serving place when you always want people to be pulled toward you instead of pushed toward their goals. So, I've decided I want to live life catapulting others toward their dreams, goals, and most importantly, God. I want to be an environment for my friends to thrive and grow.

Finally, let's look at the scene set in these verses: "Every day they continued to meet together in the temple courts. They broke bread in their homes and ate together with glad and sincere hearts, praising God and enjoying the favor of all the people. And the Lord added to their number daily those who were being saved" (Acts 2:46-47). The early church broke bread and ate together in their homes. We all know there is something personal about having dinner with friends. We could say that we are sustaining life together. We should be intentional to have get-togethers that cheer us on in life and our walk with God.

I love how verse 46 says, "with glad and sincere hearts, praising God and enjoying the favor of all the people." We know that we should be sincere with our relationships, but it is embarrassing how many relationships I've had over the years that were disingenuous. Relationships can become obligations, requirements, or worse, stepping-stones. Have you ever used someone to get to the next person, next position, or for the advancement of your agenda? Or maybe you needed a relationship because of insecurity in your life, or you expected someone to give you identity, something only God can do. These scenarios can cause people to be false securities in our life. When they can't sustain the weight of demands placed on them, both parties are left empty in their need for fellowship.

As a result of situations like these, we lack the authenticity needed to praise God, enjoy favor, and attract others to Jesus.

Sincerity brings favor as shown at the end of verse 47. They were praising God and enjoying the favor of all the people, enjoying the favor of their friendships. When we have favor with one another, we have access to each other's gifts, skills, and abilities. I love having access to Kate's take on life, her experiences, and her time with God. I can't help but become closer to her and God when she shares her knowledge with me. This has happened with other close friends as well. When we've made ourselves vulnerable, set aside insecurities and comparison, and made time to grow with each other, we have nourished beautiful friendships that will stand the test of time and the test of awkward Bible studies.

Now it's up to you to create with Jesus. First, read Acts 2 and take note of what you appreciate about the early church. Then, think of ways you can cultivate community. Here are some ideas to jumpstart your journey:

- Start a Bible study group and read the Bible together. You don't need to teach or preach or know a lot to read the Bible and simply talk about what it means.

- Invite a friend to coffee for a thoughtful conversation about the Lord.

- Be intentional with the friends you have. Invite someone over for dinner and sustain life together.

- Join a small group or volunteer at your church, not to check something off a list, but to get to know new people and purposefully engage.

THERE ARE TIMES
WHEN BEING KIND
IS CONVENIENT, IT'S
EASY, AND IT MAKES
SENSE. BUT MANY
TIMES, BEING KIND
IS INCONVENIENT,
CHALLENGING,
OR COMPLETELY
ILLOGICAL.

CHAPTER THREE
Live in Kindness

Jacksons - Family of 6

Elaina - Family of 3

Parkers - Family of 4

Michaels – Family of 2

Perry – Single Rider

April – Single Rider

Marleys - Family of 3

Williamsons - Family of 3

THESE ARE ALL FAMILIES WHO LIVED IN my parents' home as I grew up. My parents took people in regularly and selflessly. It was never with strings attached, never as a way to hold something over their heads. Never to be able to call in a favor or because it was the right thing to do. But always because God spoke to their hearts, because my parents' home was God's home.

It was a summer day after a ten-hour shift at work. My dad pulled in the driveway in his Ford F-150 pickup. A man and his family were sitting on the pump house in the front yard. The guy's name was Tom Jackson. He had a wife and four kids. Dad instantly knew they were in a bad situation. Tom was there to ask my dad if his family could live at our house for a while. At that moment, while staring at Tom through the windshield of the F-150, the thought that gripped my dad's mind was, "You're not staying in my house, Tom." God instantly chased after that thought with, "Your house, Rodney? This is My house. You are to maintain it for me. It's My house, Rodney." Our home wasn't given to God just for Bible studies; it was His every day of the week.

Dad parked the truck, got out, and talked with Tom. He and his family moved in that day. About a month earlier, Tom had prayed that God would provide a place to live. My parents quickly adjusted our bedroom and living situation to make room. We didn't have enough rooms or bathrooms for this many people. A front entryway became my sleeping quarters for a few months, and this wouldn't be the only time I'd be displaced. In the coming years of my life, we'd find ourselves overcrowded, squeezed together, and creative with our floor plan.

One Sunday, a lady came to the altar at the church to pray. She and her two daughters were getting kicked out of her brother's home. She had no place to go. Her husband was in Germany. The plan was for her and the kids to move to Germany with him, but they weren't financially able to do that yet. So, Elaina prayed with a lady named Georgina, my mom. Mom talked to Dad, then Mom and Dad spoke to us kids. She and her daughters moved in. I don't remember too much

I grew up in a four-bedroom ranch with one bathroom. The house had two front doors. The one we always used led into a landing right off the kitchen. The other front door had a tiny foyer then went into the living room. Over time it became a storage room for goodies. When the Jacksons moved in with us, the entryway became my new bedroom. Mom and Dad made the room reassignment sound awesome, and I was excited about the change. We put a curtain over the window and deadbolted the door shut. My dresser and twin-size bed squeezed in, and we hung a curtain for my door. It was like my own New York apartment. It was sweet for about four days.

It's strange the random moments our minds file away as memories. Jake Jackson was the oldest boy, and we were about the same age. For whatever reason, I was mad at him. So, at school in art class, I drew a picture of Garfield the cat with a thought bubble saying, "Jake's a dork." It turned out great. So great that I posted it on the front of my dresser. My mom came in to put my laundry away and saw it. She laid into me about how mean it was and made me throw it away. I was roasting mad.

The biggest downside to my room being the foyer was that ridiculous curtain door. Try slamming a curtain when you want to prove a passive-aggressive point. You can't. It just comes off passive. You are the only aggressive thing, but no one knows it because the curtain denies you the satisfaction of the finality that comes with whipping your bedroom door shut.

about them, but I will never forget one particular trip to the grocery store. I was sitting in the car after a grocery shopping trip with my mom, Elaina, and one of her daughters. Mom bought me a Snickers, and the girl asked if she could eat a stick of butter, and she did. So, we sat there in the parking lot of the grocery store, gobbling down nougat and butter, the American Dream.

God used our home to provide for numerous families. Kate and I now own my childhood home and we can feel the presence of God that was invited here by my parents. We have set the purpose of our home to be a safe place. We learned from my parents' example to follow God's guidance in 1 Peter 4:9, "Offer hospitality to one another without grumbling" (NIV). We have had friends and family stay with us, and it always marks our lives, not just our walls. My cousin moved home from Arizona because of a job transfer. While he went away for training, his wife and three boys stayed with us. Another time Kate's sister, Allison, lived in Mexico. She would come home to visit and would stay with us for weeks at a time. The last time Allison stayed was for a month. Al passed away a month after leaving the last time she stayed with us. We never would've had so much time with her if she hadn't been under our roof. These times are not only about obedience and connection but also about seeking to find what God is teaching us through the people and situations He puts in our path.

Sharing our home and our life with others taught me these three things:

> First, be the kindness of Christ.
> Second, opportunities always present themselves.
> Third, God hears us when we pray.

This passage shows us how God looks at kindness to others:

> When the Son of Man comes in his glory, and all the
> angels with him, he will sit on his glorious throne. All the
> nations will be gathered before him, and he will separate

the people one from another as a shepherd separates the sheep from the goats. He will put the sheep on his right and the goats on his left.

Then the King will say to those on his right, "Come, you who are blessed by my Father; take your inheritance, the kingdom prepared for you since the creation of the world. For I was hungry and you gave me something to eat, I was thirsty and you gave me something to drink, I was a stranger and you invited me in, I needed clothes and you clothed me, I was sick and you looked after me, I was in prison and you came to visit me."

Then the righteous will answer him, "Lord, when did we see you hungry and feed you, or thirsty and give you something to drink? When did we see you a stranger and invite you in, or needing clothes and clothe you? When did we see you sick or in prison and go to visit you?"

The King will reply, "Truly I tell you, whatever you did for one of the least of these brothers and sisters of mine, you did for me." (Matthew 25:31-40 NIV)

Be the kindness of Christ.

What are reasons you've skipped showing kindness to someone?

My kindness meter runs off three things: convenience, difficulty, and logic. I want to get away from using these criteria because they are problematic and selfish. There are times when being kind is convenient, it's easy, and it makes sense. But many times, being kind is inconvenient, challenging, or completely illogical.

What is it to be the kindness of Christ? It's consistent, non-situational, and defies logic. It means we don't look at a "situation" using a meter to calculate what it will cost us. Maybe we don't even see there is a situation at all. Instead, we make ourselves available to pour out the best thing we've ever received: Love.

I believe that being kind is an on-ramp for love. They are linked together, and kindness leads us to love God and love people. Romans 2:4 reminds us of the kindness God has shown us, "Or do you show contempt for the riches of his kindness, forbearance and patience, not realizing that God's kindness is intended to lead you to repentance?" (NIV). His kindness leads us directly to the person who is Love, Jesus.

Let's look at how Jesus responds when a man asks him about eternal life:

> One day an expert in religious law stood up to test Jesus by asking him this question: "Teacher, what should I do to inherit eternal life?"
>
> Jesus replied, "What does the law of Moses say? How do you read it?"
>
> The man answered, "'You must love the Lord your God with all your heart, all your soul, all your strength, and all your mind.' And, 'Love your neighbor as yourself.'"
>
> "Right!" Jesus told him. "Do this and you will live!" (Luke 10:25-28 NLT)

I love the wording of the man's answer: with your heart, soul, strength, and mind. Or, in terms of my meter, we could say love without regard to convenience, difficulty, and logic. Our heart consists of our mind, will, and emotions. And our soul is the human part of us, our personality. Together, our heart and soul will live out what we believe.

How deeply or intensely we believe in something will determine how convenient something will be. For example, the thoughts and beliefs I have about Kate run very deeply in my heart. Therefore, her needs are convenient to me. If Kate called me stranded across the state, I would get her without suggesting a more suitable option. I want my commitment to Jesus to be the same. If He is asking me to do something, I want to respond. The question of showing kindness with our heart and soul isn't a question of our belief, faith, or heart for people; it's a question of our heart for Jesus. Kindness will be convenient because it comes from our love for Jesus.

Loving God with all our strength addresses the difficulty. Again, I have given my strength to Kate. Whether she needs me to open a jar for her or carry an emotional burden with her, she gets all I have. With access to all my strengths, she has access to all my abilities. Let's give God access to our abilities. Let's allow Him to use our strengths in showing kindness to others.

Loving God with all our mind addresses logical decisions. Kate and I are mentally connected. We want the same things. I support her dreams and goals, and we communicate about life with each other. She is on my

> It's the kindness of Christ that leads us to repentance. Kindness is a characteristic of the fruit of the Spirit, which is love. Kindness is an opportunity to activate the fruit of the Spirit in our lives. Love, joy, peace, patience, kindness, goodness, faithfulness, gentleness, and self-control are the avenues to offer love to our God, ourselves, and our neighbors.

mind a lot. So, it's logical to be with Kate and learn what she is into, up to, or wants to do. In the same way, Jesus wants to be so connected to us that it's natural for us to make mental decisions leading to kindness and compassion for others.

This expert in religious law in Luke saw and asked about a situation (getting eternal life) and wanted a measurement of the cost. His question was, "What do I need to do?" In other words, how much of me do I need to give and believe? How convenient to me will your answer be? How hard is this going to be? Does this make sense with what I'm doing? He wanted to know what the meter was and the acceptable level of love and kindness he'd need to give. But in his response, he shows that he knows there is no meter; it's *all* your heart, soul, strength, and mind. When we use a meter, our ability to love is limited. We establish mental and physical barriers to love.

So, how do we get away from metered kindness? How do we get to a place where we abandon calculating difficulty, convenience, and logic? How do we choose to be compassionate in all situations instead of avoiding some circumstances altogether? To begin to live as Christ instructed? How do we let kindness lead us into loving God and loving others?

We find answers in these verses from Titus:

> But— When God our Savior revealed his kindness and love, he saved us, not because of the righteous things we had done, but because of his mercy. He washed away our sins, giving us a new birth and new life through the Holy Spirit. He generously poured out the Spirit upon us through Jesus Christ our Savior. Because of his grace he made us right in his sight and gave us confidence that we will inherit eternal life. (Titus 3:4-7 NLT)

Kindness becomes consistent, non-situational, and beyond reason as we live in gratitude for the love Christ revealed to us through His generous mercy. He is not asking us to feel used, abused, or trampled on in the name of being kind to others. He is not asking us to be a disgruntled martyr. When my parents took people in, they may have done it out of obedience, but they lived out every situation with thankfulness.

God calls us to a life of kindness through thankfulness. We live in gratitude, knowing that Jesus never had a kindness meter toward us. With full appreciation for Him, we can love God with all our heart, soul, mind, and strength and freely love our neighbor as ourselves. We do nothing to earn His love, and there's nothing others need to do to deserve our love either. So instead of seeing kindness as sacrificial, let's choose to see kindness as a generous act of surrender.

If we look at the areas in our life where we are most thankful, we will see a surrendered heart. To surrender means to give in. Surrender is a choice, not an obligation. For example, I am extremely grateful to my wife, parents, and friends, so I find joy in showing them kindness. I will give of myself for their needs.

Total gratitude leads to total surrender. As our heart gives in to the needs of others, we begin to love unconditionally. In other words,

We acquire things in life that bring us pride and joy. Our homes can be one of those things. Kate and I revamped my childhood home and have lived in it since we've been married. My grandfather built it, and four generations have grown up in it. Our hearts are grateful for this place. It's old and has some weird quirks, but the neighbors make it all worthwhile. My mom and dad live right next door. So, it's priceless to watch Bear walk through the backyard, jump the chain-link fence instead of using the gate, and go to his grandparents' house.

like Jesus: And "Greater love has no one than this: to lay down one's life for one's friends" (John 15:13 NIV).

How much of your life are you willing to lay down? I've always read John 15:13 and thought I should be ready to die for the people I love, and maybe so. But perhaps this is talking about life more than death. Am I willing to share my home as my parents did so often? Am I willing to share a meal? To be a listening ear to a hurting friend? Am I willing to surrender family time or an anticipated vacation to be available to show kindness? Living in gratitude leads to a life laid down for others.

But it's hard to give what we haven't received. One obstacle to kindness can come from believing we don't deserve His sacrifice or forgiveness. This thought doesn't come from humility; it comes from pride. Pride causes us to think we are unforgivable or unworthy based on our merits. But it fails to consider Christ. Likewise, the inability to accept forgiveness reduces God to be less than our sins against Him. Sometimes we get to such a place of brokenness we believe God can't help us.

There's a saying, "All I have left is my pride." We cannot live with this saying rooted in our hearts. We are all a reflection of God by His design. And He isn't proud or boastful. He doesn't keep a record of wrongs for His children. Do you know what destroys pride? Not humility but gratefulness. Thankfulness. Lack of kindness can result from pride, originating from a lack of appreciation for what Jesus did for us.

Stop now to consider this: do you have a meter for showing kindness? Is it similar to what mine was? Has pride ever kept you from receiving Christ's kindness and showing it to others?

Are you intentional in finding ways to be kind?

Let's get back to our first Scripture reference In Matthew 25: 35-37:

> "For I was hungry and you gave me something to eat, I was thirsty and you gave me something to drink, I was a stranger and you invited me in, I needed clothes and you clothed me, I was sick and you looked after me, I was in prison and you came to visit me" (NIV).

> Then the righteous will answer him, "Lord, when did we see you hungry and feed you, or thirsty and give you something to drink?" (NIV)

Hungry. Thirsty. Stranger. Naked. Sick. Imprisoned. These adjectives describe every man at some point in life, physically or spiritually. We have soul needs along with physical needs. The opportunity to be kind will take us and those we are helping from hunger to feasting. From dehydration to overflowing. From a stranger to a family. From sick to made whole. From imprisonment to freedom.

That seems like a lot of opportunities. But sometimes, they can seem hard to find.

It's fascinating to me that the righteous answer Jesus in this verse by asking, "when did we see you hungry and feed you, or thirsty and give you a drink?" Did it become a part of their nature, so they didn't notice?

What is probably more likely to be true is that we lack intentional kindness. But growth, development, and effectiveness are intentional. Jesus did what He saw the Father doing, and He did it on purpose.

How many times have I said, "Man, if I only knew..."

If I knew I was being graded, I would have tried harder.

If I knew it was for you, I would have done more.

If I knew it would be like that, I would have gone, or I would have stayed home.

If I only knew Jesus was the one in need...

We can easily miss opportunities without intention. So how do we find opportunities? Before addressing this question, let me share two failed kindness attempts. These are true between Sunday stories that made me feel like an idiot who doesn't hear God.

First: French fries from Jesus.

Kate and I were on our way home from a Wednesday night church service. We were coming up to a stoplight that had two campers pulled over. The one had the hood up, so we knew there was trouble. I saw some kids sitting in the backseat of the truck and realized Kate and I needed to step in and help. But the truth is I'm not a mechanic, and my Taurus couldn't tow them, so I suggested, "Let's go to McDonald's and buy them some French fries." The train my thought was railing on was, "What parent wouldn't be thankful to have hot fries from McDonald's for their kids as they were stressed out about towing fees and mechanic costs?" I told Kate, "I think Jesus wants us to do this."

Kate, on the other hand, stated, "Do you think this will be weird?" (I guess she has a weirdness meter of her own.)

I quickly and gently corrected her lack of spiritual astuteness and said, "Babe, I really think God wants us to do this."

She said, "Okay." I kicked the Taurus in manual mode, used the paddle shifters, and blasted us to the nearest Micky

D's. At 8:20 p.m., there was a lineup. *Come on, America, we are better than that. Go home and go to bed. There is no reason to be slamming double quarter pounders that late.* So, we anxiously waited in line, my palms were sweating, and I was rehearsing in my mind how I was going to lead these families to the Christ.

I imagined it would probably be a real prodigal son moment, so I planned to ask for extra napkins to dry the tears of the newly saved. We finally ordered and jetted back to the stranded caravan of weary travelers. We broke over the hill to go down the bridge. They were gone. Not a trace of them. Not even tire tracks. Just a stupid stoplight. We had five orders of French fries in a bag. I was so irritated. Then Bear asked for a fry, so I gave him some. I made Kate eat one, and I ate the rest. As we drove home, I told Kate in all my embarrassment that I thought for sure the idea was Jesus,' not mine. But there I was eating three medium fries at 8:53 p.m., blowing my calorie intake out of the water in Jesus' name. It made no sense to me.

> What good parent would take a sack of fries from a weirdo at 8:30 p.m. under the premise that Jesus told me to buy them McDonald's? This thought never crossed my mind. If I reverse the roles and some meatball showed up with a bag of saggy, warm fries, I'd probably tell him to keep the fries and bring me a mechanic.

I put the car back in normal drive with grease-covered fingers and puttered on home, stuffing my face to keep my shame hidden. It turns out the napkins would be drying my own tears.

Second: Coffee? Table for none.

Kate and I talked one evening about not being selfish and doing something for people who were in a worse spot than we were. After an hour and a half of pumping each other up, I screamed, "Let's save someone," and rallied the family into the car. Off we went toward town to be nice to someone. The only idea we had was to buy coffee for someone suffering from low caffeine. So, I said, "We will pull into Tim Hortons and pay for the car behind us." It was going to be spiritual for everyone involved. I turned onto 24th Street and headed to Tim

Hortons, a popular coffee chain in Michigan. As I turned on the street, there wasn't a single car driving on it. I pulled into the drive-through of the coffee shop and waited. We waited for five minutes, but no one came. So, I said, "Let's head over to the Tim Hortons on Pine Grove" and off we went. We got there and the same thing—no one. Then I said, "Someone's getting a coffee tonight whether they want it or not."

I committed to going down by the boardwalk to find a homeless guy. Surely a homeless guy would be grateful for a

blazing hot coffee at 9 p.m. on a warm summer night. Oh, and did I mention? Bear had dressed up in his superhero outfit for our mission to help someone. This is embarrassing to write, but this is what happened. I couldn't scare up a homeless person for the life of me that night. We drove all over town looking for someone. Had the rapture taken place? We went home defeated. We thought we were going to be kind and uplifting to someone but found no souls in need. We got back home after 9 p.m. and tucked Bear into bed. Then, we slumped down on the couch, feeling dumb about what we had just done.

I've told these stories to people, and I've heard multiple Christianly explanations to answer these fails. But no matter how you cut the dice, that's what they were: failed attempts to

"You listened to God, and that's all He wanted." That was one explanation I received when I shared our failed attempts. Being obedient is important, and that statement is helpful to encourage. But the specifics were my choice. He said to be the kindness of Christ. I don't want to confuse the two because if I think God told me to get French fries and coffee, I'll feel like I heard His voice wrong. If I then keep failing at "God ideas," I will begin to doubt that I hear the voice of God at all. 2000 years ago, God instructed us to love our neighbor as ourselves—that's what I was obeying. I heard and followed His Word in my heart, not His voice in my head, and in that, I was successful. But if I'm honest, it was my idea to get French fries and buy coffee; that was the vehicle I chose to try to show love to others. I hitched the vehicle I chose to God's kindness wagon. I was practicing how to find an opportunity instead of waiting for one or thinking things through. I was learning.

show kindness. I know all of you want to come to my emotional rescue, explaining where God was in both of these endeavors. But I believe I have found the actual answer. We tried to find an opportunity, but it didn't work out because we were learning. We consciously stopped our daily grind and looked up. The more we've paused to look around and locate an opportunity, the better we've become at showing kindness.

So how do you see opportunities? The answer isn't profound: you look for them. I learned from those two stories that I haven't been intentional about showing kindness and love. We should look for opportunities in our scope of life, in our community of people, and in the places we frequent. It's like when you purchase a car. As soon as you own it, you see that type of vehicle everywhere. We will find what we are looking for, and if we are looking for opportunities to be kind, we will find them.

After coffee for no one, a neighbor showed up at my front door asking me about our church. He wanted to come and needed a friend to sit with. I felt like God was throwing me a bone for trying. It enriched my heart to be able to go to church with him. Opportunities are everywhere. Some come and knock on our front door; others we need to find. At the end of the day, we need to be purposeful with every opportunity to show the kindness of Christ and lead people to Love.

God hears us when we pray.

Do you struggle to believe that God is listening to you?

I can see two sides of the coin relating to prayer. One side is we pray for an answer, and the other side is that we may be the answer. You hear people joke, "Be careful what you pray for; you just might get it." This might be true.

Elaina was a mess and came to God for help. She prayed with a woman she didn't know. At that moment, she had no idea she was holding hands with her answer. Likewise, my mom didn't think she was holding hands with an opportunity. But my mom saw the need. She stopped and looked up. On that day, Mom was non-situational, beyond logical, and consistent. She lined up her life with God. Sometime after they'd let her live with us, my parents found out the reason Elaina had to leave her brother's home. It turns out she was trying to hire someone to kill him—plot twist.

Go back to that story about Tom and his Jackson Five. They moved into my parents' house for three to four months. Rewind that story some more, and you find out that one day my dad was volunteering at the church doing drywall when a lady came bursting in. She needed my dad to pray with a guy named Tom who needed a house for his family. Like all good Christians, Dad said, "Ah... ok." So, he went and prayed to God for the Jacksons to find a house. And God said, "Ah.... ok." God answered. An opportunity presented itself on a pump house, in a yard, on a summer day. On that day, my dad was non-situational, beyond logical, and consistent. He lined up his life with God. After Tom had stayed with us a few months, Dad found out Tom was sneaking out of the house while everyone was asleep. He was addicted to gambling, porn, and drinking.

When people hear the facts about our two houseguests, they naturally think it was a bad idea to let them stay in our home. It would seem dangerous for Mom and Dad to expose us kids to people like Elaina and Tom. It looked irresponsible. What if something happened to our family? If people didn't say it, I'm sure some were thinking it. Convenience, difficulty, and logic ask those questions, create those statements, and excuse the love of God. However, my parents weren't leading us toward danger. They were leading us toward God's love.

Don't get me wrong. My parents always set expectations and ground rules for our guests. It wasn't long before my dad had a serious talk with Tom, and they set an appropriate deadline for him to find a permanent living situation. God's love isn't irresponsible, but it responds appropriately when you're sensitive to the Holy Spirit.

God heard the prayers of the Jacksons and Elaina and every other family who shared our home. And He answered. He answered the prayers of my parents too. Looking back, I can see that my parents were the LIVE-Ins. They lived in God's house. They lived in God's kindness. They lived in His opportunities, and they lived in their prayers. I'd love to hear Jesus call Rodney and Georgina Thompson's names and tell them, "Whatever you did for one of the least of these brothers and sisters of mine, you did for me." Mostly so I could lean over to the angel next to me and say, "I'm not trying to brag, but I kind of know those guys."

I CAN IMAGINE
FATHER GOD SAYING
THIS TO YOU AND
ME. IN HIS MOST
SINCERE DAD VOICE,
HE SPEAKS TO US,
"YOU WERE BORN
TO BE GREAT. THE
WORLD NEEDS YOU
TO BE GREAT. I
DESIGNED YOU TO
BE GREAT."

CHAPTER FOUR

Your Greatness

BEGINNING WITH ELEMENTARY SCHOOL, I was a bother to anyone who had authority over me. I was not a fan of being told what to do. I guess I preferred to be asked. As an adult, I still like to be asked to do something, but who doesn't? I used to think it was in middle school that my academic train derailed, but I came across my report cards from Indian Woods Elementary and realized I never even boarded the "good grades train." Elementary report card: Nathan does not apply himself. Nathan daydreams. Nathan talks too much. Nathan still doesn't apply himself. Nathan doesn't manage his time appropriately. Nathan's the worst; keep Nathan home.

In fourth grade, I made it to the top ten in a spelling bee. I was standing in front of the library with the nine other geniuses of my day. Our classmates were all jealous of our brilliance as we spelled words like "butter," "needle," and "scissors." I remember my teacher, Mrs. Yang, staring at me in disbelief, shaking her head, surely thinking, "What the heck is Nathan doing up there?" Of course, I didn't know what I was doing up there either, but I sure was enjoying the moment of feeling like one of the smart kids. I was immediately relieved of my prestigious position as a top contender on the first word given. I wish so badly I could remember what the word was.

I knew I was not keeping up with my classmates academically but didn't grasp how I could. My peers just seemed to do the homework and have the answers when called on. I excelled in art class, gym, and going home. By fifth grade, I spent 90% of my recesses in the classroom doing homework or catching up on the day's work that I fell behind on.

By sixth grade, my dad dropped me off at school an hour early for math tutoring. I can remember the teacher was a very tall woman with straight black hair. I knew she wasn't the type to be trifled with. At 06:30 a.m., she was all business and I was half asleep. She ate kids like me for breakfast. She probably worked at Hogwarts before Chippewa Middle School.

My parents tried their best to keep me on track for passing each grade. Now that I'm older, I'm confident I would have wanted to punch me in the face if I was one of my teachers. So, thank you to all my teachers who held back and just kicked me out of your class or graciously passed me along to the next grade instead. Then, during the summers between 6th and 8th grade, I was

In fourth-grade art class, I dedicated the whole hour to creating a fake pack of cigarettes. They turned out amazing. No adult in my life smoked except my neighbor. I don't know what compelled me to make my pack of smokes, but I was ready to fake light one up on the playground. A couple of friends saw my creativity and asked to bum a cig. I gave them away freely, feeling like a real "people's champion." Jenny pretended to light one up in the middle of class. She was immediately told to throw it away and ratted out her pusher to save her own skin. All my contraband was confiscated, and I just stared at the back of Jenny's head the rest of the day, planning my next move.

grounded consecutively for catching my neighbor's house on fire, and then catching my sister's clothes on fire. I wasn't a pyromaniac; I just thought fire was neat. Being a country boy, I had enough time on my hands to be curious. I thought my experiments were creative and resourceful, but my parents were not impressed.

The last spanking I received from my dad happened about two weeks into the summer vacation after sixth grade. After my cousin, Mark, and I put out the fire on the neighbor's porch from our firecracker, I walked home alone. Mark refused to come with me. I entered the house, and Dad said, "Go to the garage," as he met me in the foyer. I knew the neighbor called the house. My eyes filled with water as if they had already experienced what was about to happen. I was confused about why we were going to the garage. Questions were racing through my mind. Finally, I realized this might be the day I met Jesus. As we walked into the garage, I broke. I began weeping. I tried to explain what had happened. But before I could get audible words out of my mouth, I was lifted into the air like aliens were abducting me. I wasn't that lucky. As I dangled like a pinata from Dad's left arm, his right hand came like a wrecking ball. I received three taps on my bottom from my very physically fit father. He then gently dropped me on the floor, leaving me in a heap of saliva and tears, closed the door behind him, and walked away. After I mustered the strength and courage to go in the house, I learned I was grounded for three months—starting immediately. My punishment brought joy to my sisters, who made it their priority to keep watch over me for the next ninety days while my parents were at work. Thanks to their keen eyes and big mouths, I wouldn't leave the yard to play with any friends the entire summer.

My teachers consistently moved me to the front of the classroom. One time in math class, I sat in the back next to my cousin. This particular day my cousin decided he would randomly punch me in my leg during the entire hour. The situation escalated quickly, and I was relocated within twenty minutes. I didn't learn any better in the front, but at least I knew what page we were on.

Within the first weeks of high school, my English teacher, Mr. Barnum, kicked me out of his class for being disruptive. Before he sent me to the office, he had a word with me in the hallway. He told me I was a leader, and when I acted up, the whole class acted up. It wasn't that I was causing trouble; more times than not, I was trying to commentate on a statement or situation to create a laugh. I was like Higgins on *The Tonight Show*. Just adding color to what might be a muted picture. I walked around the halls for the rest of that hour because I didn't know where the offices were, and I wasn't going out of my way to find them.

I was kicked out of art class four years in a row by Mrs. Smith. My older cousin, Dave, had gone through her art class years ahead of me and was a bit of an artist, and he applied himself. Mrs. Smith loved Dave. When she found out he was my cousin, she loved me too. The kind teacher saw the same potential in me, but I didn't care and her love for me faded. One time she said I was a complete waste of talent and to get out of her class, to which I replied, "I'll see you next year."

In 11th grade, I was on pace to not graduate. My school guidance counselor called me into his office. He leaned back in his chair, folded his hands, and said, "Mr. Thompson, Mr. Thompson, what are we going to do with you?" I just sat there thinking, "I don't know what to do with me either."

We were in Mr. Harson's math class. It's not crucial to the story, but he looked oddly similar to Mr. Burns from The Simpsons. As all the students quietly worked on the math lesson, my cousin and I had different objectives. He kept trying to punch me in the shin, while my attention was drawn to a more personal endeavor.

I had itched the side of my nose and noticed a sharp poke from some dried nasal mucus. So, in the privacy of my own desk space, I decided to do a little search and rescue. What happened next changed my life forever. I latched on to what I thought was a run-of-the-mill, everyday typical rock-hard dust bunny booger. What I pulled out of my head that morning would have killed a lesser man. The simplest description? It looked like a dehydrated avocado. I just sat there staring in awe and wonder. Was I okay? Did I just remove my gallbladder? Would I still be able to have kids? There was no way to know. But I did know there was pain radiating from my shin. Being pulled from my trance, I swung back and yelled at my cousin, "Knock it off!" I lost my grip and the booger launched from my hand like a rocket leaving Cape Canaveral. It stabbed him in the temple, then landed on his shoulder. Time stood still. I gazed at it like I was watching a family of ducklings cross a busy freeway. So many directions this could go. As he lifted the projectile off his shoulder to identify the U.F.O., I found myself in a bit of a conundrum. Part of me wanted it back for scientific reasons; the other part didn't want him to discover what type of treasure just smoked him in the face. He figured it out somewhat quickly and was not happy with what he found. But as he was getting ready to release the Kraken, Mr. Harson stepped in. Right before the booger hit the fan, I received a new desk right next to the teacher. I was safe for now.

Some fun situations my parents were troubleshooting between Sundays were:

- One day I chopped a spray paint can in half with a machete. I covered myself, along with the siding, in black paint. My dad decided gasoline would remove the paint the easiest. He did love me. I think he was trying to prove a point because it's cold-blooded to use gasoline on someone's skin.

- I locked Cheryl in a chicken coop with a rooster. She has a scar to remind her roosters are the modern-day Raptor and should be treated with respect.

- I was a founder in gathering the neighborhood gents together for BB gun wars. After someone had a BB stuck in their ear and some of us got shot in the face, we called it quits.

My cousins Mark and Andy had a huge barn behind their house. We climbed up the rafters and strung a rope from the top corner to the opposite wall. Then, we found a pully that looked like it helped hoist the sails of the Mayflower. After cutting the end of a hockey stick for a handle, I fastened it with a couple of nails to the pully, and voila, we had a zip line. As the rope sagged across the length of the barn, I saluted my fellow soldiers. Then, I leaped out of the rafters like a trapeze artist. I descended straight down the first four feet until the rope tightened. Then came a ten-foot drop due to the faulty engineering of the handle construction. Come to find out, three finishing nails can't support the jolt of force eighty-two pounds create when free falling to the earth. I pretty much fell sixteen feet to the flatbed trailer my uncle used to haul hay. There wasn't any hay on it at the time of impact. It hurt, and I cried.

I liked to tinker and get into stuff. And I had some creative abilities. I still enjoy making things, but I stick with woodworking or songwriting. Thankfully, no one ever got injured besides Cheryl and me. I did have some close calls, but maybe God was looking out for me in my stupidity.

During the eighteen years it took to graduate from high school, my parents did their best to help me. They sought out tutors and went to every teacher-parent conference. And as a result of the debacles mentioned previously, I endured many spankings and spent a few good summers grounded.

Throughout my childhood, one of the most common ways my dad would greet me was by saying, "Hello, your greatness." Other times he'd call me "Nate the great" or "my little genius."

And he'd say things like, "Oh great one; What are you doing?" My parents knew me well with all my shortcomings. So, of all the people in my life, my parents had the most reason to call me names and use hurtful words to describe me. But instead, these were the words they chose. As an adult, I wondered if my dad used those phrases sarcastically, but they never felt that way as a kid. I've always been sharp, witty, and ready. If my dad were condescending, I would've picked up on it.

We all have our own war stories of childhood. I guarantee some people have stories that are far more adventurous and challenging than mine. Through all life's experiences, we have been called names. We've also given names to others that weren't on their birth certificate. So, ask yourself, what names were you given as a child? What names outline your identity? Now compare those names to who God says you are.

- We are made in His image. (Genesis 1:27)

- We are His workmanship, created for good works. (Ephesians 2:10)

- We are chosen by Him, royal, and holy. (1 Peter 2:9)

- We are His children, sons, and daughters. (1 John 3:1, 2)

- We are new creations. (2 Corinthians 5:17)

- We are conquerors. (Romans 8:37)

- We are loved. (John 3:16)

My parents have never called me a degrading name. That may be impossible for some people to believe, but it's true. They never said, "You're an idiot, "dummy," "Why can't you learn," "You're stupid," "You're going to be a loser when you grow up," "You're an absolute waste," or anything like that.

I remember dad picking me up from that meeting with my counselor in 11th grade. On the outside, I was a funny guy who didn't care too much about school, but inside, the realization that I might be the only one of my siblings and cousins not to graduate was settling in. When I got in the car, my dad started telling me how I scored exceptionally high in problem-solving on a test I took in primary school. Dad went back to the beginning. He reminded me how my score was "off the charts." I remember thinking, "Dad, I was ten years old, and currently, I'm not solving any problems." To him, I was still a "little genius." Don't get me wrong; he was not impressed with getting me from school after the meeting with the counselor.

We tend to become who people say we are, especially when listening to people whose words carry weight in our lives. The weight of labels from influential people can tip the scales from who God says we are. God's Word tells us the importance of how we think about ourselves. In Proverbs 23:7 we read, "For as he thinks in his heart, so he is" (NKJV). So, who are you believing? Him or them?

I learned the importance of three types of expressions from how my parents spoke to me:

First, the declaration.

Second, the catalyst.

Third, the potential.

The declaration

Whose words have shaped your identity?

Our words carry the weight of life and death as we learn in Proverbs 18:20, 21,

"Wise words satisfy like a good meal; the right words bring satisfaction. The tongue can bring death or life; those who love to talk will reap the consequences." (NLT)

We forget how heavy words are. And it's a bummer that often the best reminder of what they can do occurs when they belittle or kill. Sticks and stones may break my bones, but words will never hurt me. Are we still saying that? Words destroy people every day. Maybe it's because life takes time to cultivate, while death can happen so swiftly. It will take twenty years for a pine tree to grow, but in five minutes, I cut it down, strap it to the roof of my Jeep, and take it home as a Christmas tree just to be dragged into my back yard and torched two months later. Rest in peace, little fella. I'll be back for another one of your buddies in ten months.

My parents could've cut me down; they were not oblivious to life. They didn't live in denial of what was happening around them or with their son. When they talked to me, they pointed me toward something bigger or more significant. They spoke life into me. They made me do my homework, grounded me from friends, spanked me good, took away my Nintendo, *and* told me I was great. They were declaring who God said I was over who others said I was. Although I'm sure 90% of the time Dad called me a "little genius" his mind had passed on other thoughts and phrases that could better describe the moment.

One experience or a single set of circumstances within a problematic season can put a lifetime label on who you are. People and society will speak into our identity based on their perception. If we do something they don't like, they call us an idiot, a screw-up, or worthless. We often build our sense of self around these false ideas. I've believed many lies because someone spoke into the moment I was in, not into the future I needed to move toward. I don't want the resolve of who I am to be based on the words of people who can quickly change their minds about me. My dad's words were consistent, regardless of my actions. My dad was echoing the voice of God even if he didn't mean to.

We need to listen to the declaration of who God says we are. One important declaration is found in Ephesians 2:10, "For we are God's masterpiece. He has created us anew in Christ Jesus, so we can do the good things he planned for us long ago" (NLT). If no one tells us we are God's masterpiece, we leave ourselves open to suggestions from people. When I was a kid, I promised that I wouldn't let anyone call me stupid. I remember my fourth-grade teacher trying to get me to answer a question in front of the class. The teacher called on me to explain, but I had another point of view. So, instead of reciting the answer she expected, I was trying to explain why my answer could be correct too. She looked at me and said, "It's like pulling teeth with you, Nathan." I didn't know what that meant, but it made me feel small. I remember I started shutting down that day.

Moments like that can kill fruit-bearing branches in our life. Jesus tells us that we are to be branches on His vine. In John 15:5 we read, "I am the vine; you are the branches. If you remain in me and I in you, you will bear much fruit; apart from me you can do nothing" (NIV).

When we believe a lie, based on who someone says we are or who we perceive ourselves to be, we remove a branch from the Vine. That branch stops growing from our true identity and life source, Jesus. Instead, we take the broken branch and connect it to the lie. We try to make it grow within the identity given to us by our peers, parents, teachers, or selves.

When we graft our branch into a lie, our false identity begins to develop. Meanwhile, the truth of our created identity dies apart from the Vine. We don't notice because as the fruit from the Vine withers, the product of the lie grows. It still looks like "life," but any product of the lie will not sustain us and eventually brings destruction. But since this is who others want us to be and who we know ourselves to be, we continue with the false identity. We hear whispers of the Father's voice calling us back, but the significant changes we'd need to make or the people we'd need to face to get back to the Vine seem overwhelming. I've let people define me, and I've had to find my way back to the Vine. But it's worth the work. When we plug back into Truth, relief comes in knowing we no longer need to perform or meet expectations. We simply pull our resources from Him.

The declaration of who we are cannot come from men. It cannot come from nurture or nature. It must come from who God says we are, or branches in our life will eventually produce no eternal fruit; they will disconnect, dry up, and die. The fruit produced from lies isn't the same as fruit produced from God's truth. It's like a mango at the grocery store during a season you shouldn't be able to get a mango. It's there and appears good but lacks flavor, juice, and ripeness. It's man-made fruit instead of God-made fruit. It doesn't represent who we are.

Identity comes from three sources: insecurity, false security, or God. Insecurities are lies, skewed ideas, or inaccurate perceptions of who we are. I believe they come from critical life moments that project us on a new path. Insecurities snuff out who God created us to be. For example, maybe God has designed you to share ideas through speaking or writing. In fourth grade, your teacher implies your unique perspective is unimportant and makes you feel small. Insecurity enters the scene and takes you for a ride in one of two directions. One, your voice doesn't matter and what you have to say is insignificant, so be quiet. Or the second, you need to be the loudest voice, and what you have to say should be valued at a premium, so everyone else shut up.

False securities are external objects like friends, spouses, leaders, entities, or careers. These facets in life can't sustain the weight of validating us. I remember hearing a conversation with a surgeon who was retiring. He casually said that if he wasn't a surgeon anymore, he didn't know who he was. False security will always be a faulty foundation. When it's removed, we find ourselves fractured or crushed and need to reevaluate our identity. Timothy Keller says, "When we build our lives on anything but God, that thing – though a good thing – becomes an enslaving addiction, something we *have* to have to be happy" (Reason for God). What do you *need* to be happy?

Insecurities and false securities can affect us for a lifetime and beyond a lifetime. In the end, we will answer to the source of our true identity. One of the biggest dangers of believing a lie is attaching ourselves to all the lies that come with it, creating an intricate web of deceit. If we pull at any strand in the web, questioning the lie, we need to examine our foundational beliefs, and life becomes confusing. We don't share portions of our hearts because we don't have confidence in what we say we believe. Buckle in for this.

If I convinced you your blue shirt is green, then when you go outside on a sunny day and see a blue sky, you would say, "That must be a green sky because it matches my shirt." You have your doubts about the color, and maybe a friend even has the same shirt as you, and they still call theirs blue and not green. If you don't go with the idea that the sky is green, you would need to reconsider what you believe about the color of the shirt. And you'd have to question everything you'd ever considered to be blue or green. You don't tell anyone that you're confused about the colors because you're afraid to challenge your long-standing beliefs about the definition of blue and green.

> Believing a lie causes you to believe all the lies attached to it. Apply this to your relationship with God. Somewhere we believed a lie about Him, and now we miss or disregard aspects of who He is because it doesn't match what we learned. Always be willing to bring questions to God. He can handle your confusion and doubts. If He couldn't, we would have a bigger problem on our hands.

You may have learned that it's wrong to question your faith or beliefs, that questioning equals doubt. But a sincere quest for answers will confirm who you are and what you believe or reveal a lie. Like Hebrews 4:12 says, "For the Word of God is living and active, sharper than any two-edged sword, piercing to the division of soul and of spirit, of joints and marrow, and discerning the thoughts and intentions of the heart" (English Standard Version). Test your identity and life against who God says you are. Then, like a skilled surgeon, He will help you separate the truth from lies.

Real identity comes from security in God, who created us in His image and likeness. He is the only one who can sustain the weight and the constant draws we make for identity validation. He knows who we are, who He created us to be, and the purpose He set on our life. God knows us and all our potential. He not only imparts our identity but confirms it often.

I can imagine Adam, at the beginning of creation, communing with God. Adam would freely cultivate and create throughout the day, exploring the creation God had entrusted to him. I can see Adam wanting to share his work and ideas with his closest companion, returning to his Creator at the end of the day. I imagine the joy God felt at all Adam had accomplished, at the beauty of His creation that had been made in His image. I picture God affirming Adam, the same way He affirms you and me. He will remind us daily that who He made is good. Us. Remember what God is declaring over you.

> Doubting Thomas or honest Thomas? Thomas had unanswered questions, and he didn't hide from them. He shared his disbelief with his friends, and they didn't call him an idiot and disown him or belittle him. Instead, in his questioning, Thomas became one of the first recorded to fall at the feet of Jesus and worship Him as the resurrected Savior.

I've taken the time to sift through declarations in life that propelled me in the wrong direction. Certain instances highlighted potential insecurities and grew them into my identity. As a child, I made a promise that I wouldn't let anyone make me feel small or stupid. As a result, I pulled in and disconnected from trying certain things, especially academics. Learning something new had to be on my terms. I relied heavily on humor to relieve the tension and cope with shortcomings.

As a grown man, I had to address these lies and resolve the truth with God. One day, during prayer, God addressed this directly in my heart. The Holy Spirit reminded me I'm in Him,

> My job is working in the Cardiovascular Labs at a hospital. When I accepted the position, one of the docs told me it would take about five years to feel comfortable in the new role. Had I not dealt with the insecurities around learning, feeling stupid would've brought the worst out of me. Instead, I learned the position to the point where I am trusted to train the new hires. God can take insecurity (my aversion to learning) and turn it into a strength (using me to teach).

and He is in me. Because of this, I will never come up short. I will never be found lacking. I will always be enough. He is the weight and scales by how I am measured now. When God sees me, He sees Jesus.

Building on insecurity and false security, I was arrogant, stubborn, and short-tempered. Building on God's foundation, knowing He is my source of creativity and fresh perspectives, I've come to enjoy learning and sharing. I've forgiven my fourth-grade teacher, who was probably on the brink of a meltdown herself dealing with the "fresh perspectives" of thirty fourth-graders. And I'm making it a point in my life to recognize when I can point other people to the source of their identity.

The catalyst

Can you think of someone who was a catalyst in your life? What direction did they send you?

catalyst–

1: a substance that enables a chemical reaction to proceed at a usually faster rate or under different conditions (as at a lower temperature) than otherwise possible

2: an agent that provokes or speeds significant change or action

Sitting on the middle cushion of the couch in our living room, I stared at the wall in a daze. I was a fresh graduate of Port Huron Northern High School. Unfortunately, I was not good at anything. I was the opposite of Liam Neeson in the movie *Taken*. I had no particular set of skills. If I found you, I wouldn't kill you. I wouldn't know what to do with you. I had no direction, idea, or passion. No plan. I was just sitting on a couch, staring at a wall.

Even with family and friends who loved me, I was the closest I've been to sinking in the quicksand of depression. I've never been clinically depressed. I've been bummed out, sad, really sad, bland, indifferent, tired, not interested, not interesting, and not engaged, but never depressed. But that day, I believe I was on the cusp.

Our bodies are programmed to compensate. I've seen it in my job as a nurse when someone's heart does a great job making up for lack of blood flow until it just can't do it anymore and a heart attack ensues. Our minds do the same type of compensation for our emotional health. It looks for places in life that it can pull joy from to make up for areas lacking. But eventually, it all of a sudden can't anymore. I think that's where I was, right smack dab in the middle of a full-blown brain attack.

Remember Proverbs 23:7, "For as a man thinks in his heart, so he is" (NKJV).

At that moment, I did not hear my dad calling me "great one." Instead, I was hearing about people from school moving on to college with a plan. Friends were out getting better jobs than me. I knew my life sucked. Thankfully, this was before social media platforms. I can't imagine if I had been scrolling on my phone through all my friends' problem-free lives. I'd be seeing their super-fit, active, constantly traveling existence. I'm not sure if jealousy or apathy would set in as I watched my peers trying new exotic foods while wearing their brand-new clothes and driving the truck I'd wanted to own for the past ten years. I'm grateful Facebook and Instagram weren't around to remind me how bad my life certainly was.

I was sitting there swirling in the toilet bowl of life, ready to be flushed, when Mom came casually cruising by putting away laundry. Probably my laundry because I was lazy. She stopped and said, "What's wrong, baby?" To appreciate that statement from Mom, you would have to hear her say it with her sweet Spanish accent. I began unloading the facts that I sucked at life and had no idea what I was going to do. School was pointless because "look where it got me," and "I'm never going to be anything useful," etc.

Mom's response to my pity and self-wallowing was, "Go read Joshua 1:9," and then she vanished like a snow leopard. I'm sure that my first thought was that it was not helpful advice. But I rolled off the couch like a sunbaked walrus falling off a rock into the ocean and found my dad's Bible. I had just turned eighteen, and God was not on my radar. But my mom was a catalyst at that moment. Like the definition, she was an agent that provoked significant change or action. She could have given me routine parent advice and said, "Quit lying there like an old sock." She could have said, "Get off your butt and do something with your life like your friends are doing. Quit being you and try to be like someone else." But I needed more than a push; I needed action. I needed a catalyst toward someone greater, toward someone who could sustain significant change. I needed a reminder of who I was; to be brought back into action by the source of identity. Opinions don't inspire sustained action, but what God says about us can.

I read Joshua 1:9, "'This is my command—be strong and courageous! Do not be afraid or discouraged. For the Lord your God is with you wherever you go'" (NLT). And after reading the Scripture, I got up and applied to three different trade schools and four colleges. Within the week, they all responded. They told me I was exactly who they'd been looking for, and I had my choice of what I wanted to pursue. But, of course, that's a lie. I didn't do that, and none of that happened.

Nothing exciting took place externally for me that day. I don't even think my mom came back to hug me or check on me. Instead, I got up and washed my car. But something did happen internally. My mom spoke life into me. She pointed me to something bigger than my view of reality, even if I didn't recognize it at the time. I read that I should not be afraid or discouraged because my mom's God, and kind of my God by default, was with me wherever I went, whether I wanted Him to be or not. And it was accurate enough at the moment to get me off the couch. When we are lost, broken, or during tragedy, God becomes more real because we are vulnerable to Him. When all the crutches we've made to help us walk through life disappear, we see how incapable we are.

It's important to mention I was vulnerable and open to a variety of input in my life. A wrong catalyst at that right time would've sent me further into insecurities and false securities. Mom didn't give me her opinion; she gave me God's Word.

Opinions change, but His Word doesn't. And soon after that moment, her God would become my God.

We all have times when we need someone to speak life into us, but we can also be a catalyst to point someone in the right direction, to remind them of their greatness. I'm sure my mom doesn't remember telling me to read Joshua 1:9. The Bible was just part of her language. She was living naturally from her identity in Christ, walking in the Spirit. That's how I want to be too.

I want to walk around seeing the possibilities in peoples' lives, encouraging them into their future, and sending the Word of God out over their lives. My mom didn't know that an insignificant moment for her was changing the world for me. When you look into the wild eyes of your kids, the indecisive teenager, a broken co-worker, or desperate neighbors and friends, speak to the infinite possibilities for their future instead of their momentary situation. Choose to share the Word of God.

The potential

Do you have more to offer life?

I think, by God's design, we have endless potential. That's a bold statement for some of us to wrap our heads around. I mean, if we just think of some of our favorite YouTube fail videos, that statement seems untrue.

We are designed to house God himself. 1 Corinthians 6:19 tell us, "Do you not know that your bodies are temples of the Holy Spirit, who is in you, whom you have received from God? You are not your own" (NIV). We were made to walk with

Him and talk with Him. We live in Him, and He lives in us. I'm not a scholar, but it seems to me that for an object to house and accommodate an infinite God, that object's potential must be as endless as what it is accommodating.

The same God who announced to the universe, "Let there be light," chose *you* to show His light to others. We read in 2 Corinthians 4:5-7, "For what we preach is not ourselves, but Jesus Christ as Lord, and ourselves as your servants for Jesus' sake. For God who said, 'Let light shine out of darkness,' made his light shine in our hearts to give us the light of the knowledge of God's glory displayed in the face of Christ. But we have this treasure in jars of clay to show that this all-surpassing power is from God and not from us" (NIV).

We shine His light by sharing who God is, and we know who God is through the man, Jesus Christ. God is the source and power behind our endless potential. And all we do should point back to Him.

We can't always believe the story we're telling ourselves. At times, we lie to ourselves about what we are capable of because we have lost sight of the potential we were created for. There have been words spoken over us, and from us, that sent us off course. Catalysts, friends, family, and trusted sources who couldn't see where God was calling us. But our tomorrows have a purpose. Tomorrows allowing us to minister back to the Lord from a uniqueness that only we can offer Him. Tomorrows full of possibilities from a limitless God who lives inside vessels like you and me.

To live in the fullness of how God created us, we need to know our identity. We need to hear it from the One who knows us inside and out.

These verses from Psalm 139:13-18 are a reminder of how God knows intimately:

> For you created my inmost being; you knit me together in my mother's womb. I praise you because I am fearfully and wonderfully made; your works are wonderful, I know that full well. My frame was not hidden from you when I was made in the secret place, when I was woven together in the depths of the earth. Your eyes saw my unformed body; all the days ordained for me were written in your book before one of them came to be. How precious to me are your thoughts, God! How vast is the sum of them! Were I to count them, they would outnumber the grains of sand— when I awake, I am still with you. (NIV)

This Scripture shows that God has been speaking greatness over us since the beginning. My dad did the same, reminding me of written proof that his son tested "off the charts," in spite of the type of son I had created myself to be. At that moment, I brushed off the fact that my father knew something about me that I didn't. But my lack of recognition didn't make his story about me untrue. There was truth written about us before we grabbed the pen and began writing. There has been a declaration made from God Himself about all of us before insecurity and false security had a chance to lower the bar for our potential.

I love how President Roosevelt's parents spoke to his potential. When he was a child, his parents told him daily, "You were born to be great. The world needs you to be great." They spoke to his possibilities, not his limitations. Kate and I ran with this statement and have said it to Bear since he was born. I can imagine Father God saying this to you and me. In

His most sincere Dad voice, He speaks to us, "You were born to be great. The world needs you to be great. I designed you to be great."

There are two sides of the identity conversation, what we are accepting and what we are declaring. We have the opportunity to speak over someone else and receive what is spoken over us, to be a catalyst in someone's life and be propelled, to speak to others' potential and understand the greatness God has placed in us. If we choose to live according to our God-given identity, we could be catalysts filling our world with security, purpose, and endless possibilities.

WHEN WE LACK
OWNERSHIP IN A
MISSION, IT'S NOT
BECAUSE WE LACK
RESPONSIBILITY
OR DESIRE; IT'S
BECAUSE WE HAVE
LOST SIGHT OF THE
END GOAL AND NEED
DIRECTION TO HELP
US REFOCUS.

CHAPTER FIVE

The Mission

L ET ME TAKE YOU BACK TO OCTOBER 31, 1987. I was six years old. It was a beautiful Halloween day around 3 p.m. The sun was shining, the colorful Michigan leaves had begun to fall, and pumpkin spice drinks weren't a thing yet. I was approaching my house while riding the school bus with my sisters. We came to the bus stop in front of our home, but today was no ordinary day. Today there were fire trucks in my yard. What American child doesn't get pumped up when a fire truck surprises them in front of their house? Everyone on the bus shifted toward the windows. There were a lot of *oooohs* and *aaaahs*. Of course, when you're an adult, fire trucks in the yard are frightening, produce anxiety, and generally come with an insurance claim. But as a kid, this was the most exciting thing to happen all year. I couldn't get off the bus fast enough to find the cause of all the commotion.

After a quick investigation by the firefighters, they discovered the furnace had trouble, and the wall behind it caught on fire. We were now temporarily homeless, but the place wasn't a total loss. Thankfully, our neighbor saw the smoke early and swiftly notified

We stayed at my aunt's house one night following the house fire. I don't remember much about it other than walking in the door holding a pillow. At some point before morning, one of my siblings fell down the stairs after using the bathroom, and the other woke up half the house, screaming, "trick-or-treat!" Houseguests are great.

the fire department before our house became an inferno. We stayed at my aunt's house the first night and then moved into a tiny trailer for the next eight months as my dad started to repair the home.

The trailer was crammed. It was the equivalent of packing five chicken breasts into a four-piece chicken McNuggets container. We celebrated Christmas and rang in the new year in our slightly used mobile home. By the way, trailers are the original tiny home. I hope they have a comeback because they're pretty ingenious if you stop to think about it. So, we went from our 2,200 square foot ranch to a 700 square foot corral. There were two rooms in the tiny tin tube, and I was in one of them for the duration of our stay. My sisters slept in the other bedroom, and my parents slept on the couch, making the best of what we had. Unfortunately, at the time of the fire, we didn't have homeowners' insurance. So, the cost of repairs fell directly on Mom and Dad. After my dad got out of work, he would go over to the house and chip away at the damaged area.

While turmoil was surrounding us in the fall of '87, my parents had a plan to address something more significant than the house fire. Mom and Dad were hatching a plan to send Mom on a three-month mission trip to her home country, Honduras, in March of 1988. My parents began planning this trip the summer before the fire and believed they still needed to move forward with the mission despite our house situation. As my parents' relationship with God grew, Mom felt drawn by God to go back to Honduras to share God's love with her family, her people. So, she planned to fly out in March, and Dad would hold down the fort with his three little gifts from the Lord: Kara, Cheryl, and me.

Dad was solo parenting a seven-year-old, eight-year-old, and ten-year-old while working as a machinist at Napa Auto. I'm pretty sure, based solely on personality, Kara was the only one who would prove to be helpful to him while mom was taking care of business. Kara was better than most at being the kind of child parents wanted. She was cooperative, cute, and caring. And she had huge brown eyes, like a baby cow, that gave her an extra dose of likability. I can only remember Kara bucking the system once in our childhood. Her only downfall is that she didn't like hotdogs. That's not even a real problem.

Being the middle child, Cheryl had her issues. I've never been able to appreciate the struggles of the middle child. They always seem to attract a little more drama than the rest of us, and I'm sure Dad had to deal with that head-on with Mom gone. Cheryl was a real "trailblazer" of sorts. I have to give her credit, though; she made my high school experience a breeze.

Now the youngest. I was what people in the business world like to call "the prized hog," the baby boy. The only boy. The golden child. The gift from above. The only one my mother prayed to God to receive. She prayed for a son and sought the Lord's face for me. She told me she was sitting in the back-

> Kara ran through the house screaming like a maniac whilst our mother gave chase to spank her. Cher and I were all but taking bets who would come out the victor. Kara had the lung capacity and stamina to outrun and dodge Mom long enough not to get a spanking. It was like watching a baby gazelle outmaneuver a seasoned lioness on the hunt. Finally, the lioness gave up and walked away. You shall live another day, little one, another day.

yard one day watching Cheryl and Kara play. As she surveyed her accomplishments in life, she realized she wasn't satisfied with her children. She realized there was a void in her life that her daughters couldn't fill. She realized she needed a son. I was the son my parents prayed for, and I was ready to do my part in our family's mission.

When March rolled in, Mom's plane left the tarmac, and Dad had his hands full for the next three months. She was gone and communication was limited. My parents began attending a new church around the time of the fire. One evening during a Wednesday night women's class before her departure, my mom shared what she and my dad planned with the group. She shared how she felt a tug on her heart to go back home, to travel around the different villages and towns where she grew up sharing the true Gospel. The good news of who Jesus is and what He did for her and for us all. She explained to the ladies that despite their current circumstances, the mission was happening. Mom got those ladies fired up that night, and they took a spontaneous offering to help the cause. They received $50 to help with the trip's expenses.

So, there we were—three kids, three months, a two-bed-room trailer, Mom and Dad on a mission. The Thompsons were ready, baby!

What three things did this mission trip show me?

First, you need a vision.

Second, the situation shouldn't compromise the mission.

Third, the mission has to be greater than you.

Do you have a vision for your family?

My parents accepted God's provides vision and direction: "When there is no clear prophetic vision, people quickly wander astray. But when you follow the revelation of the word, heaven's bliss fills your soul" (Proverbs 29:18 The Passion Translation). They had a clear conviction from God that He would bring this trip to fruition, and they'd begun to put some basic plans in place. They decided my mom would go alone, and my dad would hold down work and the home front. While Dad was at work, the kiddos were in school from about 8 a.m. to 3 p.m. The three of us went to the same elementary school and rode the bus together. Dad started work the same time we started school and got home a couple hours after us, so when we didn't go to Grandma's, Kara was in charge. The 120-minute window of mayhem was well controlled because Santa brought me a Nintendo for Christmas that year. I mean, that seems like a solid plan, right?

My birthday was one of the first major celebrations that took place after Mom left. Dad handled the arrangements. In hindsight, my seventh birthday had a dad's touch. No party. He made a cake with chocolate frosting and didn't wrap my presents. His clever way of dodging out of wrapping was acting as though he hid them. He told me my gift was outside. I ran out the door like a four-wheeler or a new puppy was waiting for me. With my imagination running wild, I shot out the door but stepped over my actual present. I yelled to my dad with a massive smile on my face, "Where is it? Where is my giant awesome present that doesn't fit in the house?" So, my dad started yelling from our toaster of a house, "Look on the porch!"

I went back to the porch and blankly stared at a Kmart bag that couldn't possibly contain my unwrapped gift. There's no way my loving, considerate father would only tie a knot with the white plastic bag handles and call it done. But yes, that's precisely the situation. Using all my might, I stretched the plastic fibers apart to create a saggy hole opening to peer through. Inside, a palm-sized Michigan State Spartans basketball and Nintendo game stared back at me. At this point, I was still slightly confused. Not only did I not play basketball, but I had never heard of the Nintendo game. And the present wasn't wrapped. I wondered if Cheryl had opened my birthday present and played with it.

Then I realized it was Mom who usually took care of the birthday details. The Nintendo game Dad bought me was called Jackal. I can see my dad strolling up to the wall of video games, somewhat overwhelmed, and picking out the least expensive game that would look appealing to a boy. The cover had two jeeps on it with explosions going off in the background. I've since come to believe an angel of the Lord led him to that game. It became my mission for the next year of my life. You couldn't save your progress in the game. You needed to sit there and commit your whole being to it. This game wasn't created for quitters; it was created for people without responsibilities. Destiny brought us together for such a time as this, and I was ready. I had what I needed —a vision and mission.

Without a destination or vision in mind for your family, you wander through life. Not to say wandering can't be enjoyable, but it does stall progress and growth. There is a saying I used to like, "An unaimed arrow never misses." It's true, but the pur-

> The first time I played Jackal, I wanted to smash my Nintendo with all my might. I drove my little green jeep all over the screen for twenty minutes, unable to go anywhere. Even writing this, I can feel the frustration I had. With elevated tension in my voice, I described to the whole house how things were going for me along with my feelings for the game. Cheryl came into the living room to see why I was so amped. She reached down and grabbed the other paddle. In my passion I yelled at her not to touch it, but to my surprise, the little brown square on the screen moved. I had it on two players and didn't know it. The brown square was the second Jeep. In her ignorance, she solved the biggest problem I had faced up to that moment. For that, I will be forever grateful.

pose of an arrow is to hit a target. The statement sounds fun, but there is no intention—only wandering.

Over the past few years, Kate and I have established a written vision for our family. Prayer and communication have been essential tools in this process. When developing or revisiting the vision statement, we consider who we are and want to become along with the skills, passions, and opportunities God has given us. The vision has served us well, helping us decide where to spend our resources and what we want to create as a family. It's like a compass, and with it, we set goals for the future.

For example, we wanted to go on a vacation with some friends one year, but after looking at our vision and seeing what God had in store for us, we backed up and decided the trip didn't fall in line with our other objectives. This was tough, but it's a practical example of how having a vision helps in decision-making and leads to more intentional living.

For more than ten years, Kate and I have had a "goals dinner" each year in December. We are purposeful about putting our objectives before us and deciding what goals from the previous year served God's vision well and which ones need to go. But then, we add new plans too. Our vision and goals are fluid with our seasons of life. They are not a rigid structure but a set of rails that keep us on the road. Here is an example of our vision:

> *Focus. Focus our hearts. Focus our time. Focus our finances. Focus our commitments. Focus our yes and our no. Now Do it. Go after it and execute our plans. Become doers. Dedicate all that we do and all that we place our hands on to glorify God.*

The following two verses are instrumental in guiding us as we create our goals:

> Proverbs 16:3, "Before you do anything, put your trust totally in God and not in yourself. Then every plan you make will succeed." (TPT)

> Proverbs 4:25-27, "Set your gaze on the path before you. With fixed purpose, looking straight ahead, ignore life's distractions. Watch where you're going! Stick to the path of truth, and the road will be safe and smooth before you. Don't allow yourself to be sidetracked for even a moment or take the detour that leads to darkness." (TPT)

Our vision doesn't completely change from year to year but grows and adapts with who God is making us. Our current vision reads:

Be available to create opportunities for people to en-counter Jesus within our sphere of influence and encourage others to do the same.

Kate and I wouldn't have developed the second statement if we didn't take the time to focus first. Creating and following a vision is practical for our marriage, schedule, and finances.

Without it, we would've easily wandered through months and years without clear direction.

When I think back on aimless times of life, they were unproductive. It was easy to spin my tires, so to speak, and not accomplish anything that required more of me than an average level of function or commitment. The most important thing I've learned from having our family vision is that it curbs comparison to my friends. I couldn't tell you the number of times Kate and I have pulled our phones out while on the back deck of our house to read our goals and to remember what we are doing to keep us from wanting what our friends are doing. Being confident in God's Word for you will relieve the tension that comes with feeling like:

- You're not doing enough.

- You're doing too much.

- You should be further along in your—family life, career, spiritual walk, education, etc.

- You're too old or too young to accomplish something.

As I mentioned earlier, Proverbs 29:18 provided guidance for my parents, and it's been important to me as well. Let me repeat it: "When there is no clear prophetic vision, people quickly wander astray. But when you follow the revelation of the word, heaven's bliss fills your soul" (TPT). In this verse, the word vision can be translated as revelation. Revelation will encourage, motivate, inspire, or maybe even convict us into action.

Gaining revelation from God about what He has for us streamlines life. It's like going from driving the backroads to jumping on the autobahn. Vision will not only guide our decisions; it will also fuel purpose. It will lead us to a mission.

The situation shouldn't compromise the mission.

What mission are you currently working toward? What situations are you waiting to change before you accept the mission?

It was the summer before the house fire when my parents decided they would go to Honduras. Their mission was found and written in clarity. Even though their situation dramatically changed, they had a vision in their mind. It was the vision that guided the decisions to lead them toward the mission. Troubles come, and troubles go; obstacles will always pop up and prevent us from moving forward. Or maybe the path leading to the mission won't look how we thought it would. And because it looks different than we imagined, we let off the gas and wait for the right situation, or bale completely.

Other times God gives us a place in a mission that originates from someone else. Because it's someone else's idea, we might hesitate to take full ownership. A few years ago, I was at Lakeside Beach with the family. My older nephews were out on the sandbar throwing a ball around. My younger niece, Elee, wanted to go out there, but she was too little to swim there by herself. Elee had a vision that led her to a mission that was bigger than she was. I heard about Elee's quest while knocking down a hot dog at the cookout. So, I said, "Elee, hop on my back like a little turtle, and I'll take you there."

I volunteered to be a part of her mission. Halfway across the 50-foot gap, I could no longer touch the bottom. Things started to get dicey. I bobbed down to find the bottom, which caused Elee to wrap her wiry legs and arms around my head and neck like a scarf I never wanted. During the underwater strangulation, I thought, "I don't want to be here anymore. I'm uncomfortable, and the situation has drastically changed. It seems like we no longer see eye to eye. This was not what I signed up for." In the moment, those thoughts were valid. But I didn't sign up for a moment; I signed up for a mission. I imagined I would swim out there like David Hasselhoff and make Elee's day. The inconvenience was apparent, and my lack of ownership was starting to surface.

It would sound utterly absurd to all of us if I bailed on eight-year-old Elee's dream and mission to get to the sandbar. Suppose I left her to swim the rest of the way alone because things changed for me. What kind of uncle would I be? It is evident in this story that I had value to offer Elee and abilities to carry out the responsibility of the position I accepted. We all have value and skills to contribute to a mission, regardless of who benefits or whose idea it was. We can't let situations compromise our involvement in the assignment or discredit the value we bring. I took ownership of Elee's vision and partnered with her mission.

Don't be discouraged if you're reading this and find that you don't have a mission of your own. If someone else is a dreamer and you aren't, when you partner with their dream, you have the opportunity to dream with them, which also makes you a dreamer (Cunnington 46-48). And you might start checking out on someone's mission if the ownership you have is faltering. When we lack ownership in a mission, it's not because we lack responsibility or desire; it's because we have lost sight of the end goal and need direction to help us refocus. This often happens when communication falls through the cracks and unity in purpose is lacking. Conversation brings clarity.

Let's get back to the beach. With some quick adjustments to the plan, Elee loosened the chokehold, and we made it to the sandbar. Mission completed. We played catch with the boys, I caught my breath, lactic acid levels returned to normal, we came up with a better plan for our return to land, and it was a great day.

When I first became a nurse, I worked in an ICU. I wanted to switch departments to go to the Cardiovascular Lab (CVL). An offer came by, but the timing wasn't right, so I declined it. Kate and I talked about the pros and cons and decided the next time an offer came along, I'd take it. We felt this new career path would be a great opportunity. It lined up with our vision and mission. About a year later, the CVL manager called and offered me a position. The dilemma was, it was part-time, 24 hours a week. That wouldn't provide enough income to support our family, so that was a problem. Suddenly the situation was beginning to compromise the mission. It didn't look or feel right. It seemed like we should pass on it and wait.

But in clarity, a year ago, we laid out the vision of what we were going to do, so I told Kate I wanted to take it. I told her I knew it didn't make sense right now, but it did when we prayed about it the year prior. She felt the same way, and we went for it. Even though we couldn't see exactly how the future would play out, we knew to focus on the vision we'd had. 2 Corinthians 4:18, tells us, "So we fix our eyes not on what is seen, but on what is unseen, since what is seen is temporary, but what is unseen is eternal" (NIV). We trusted God to be working, even when we couldn't see exactly what was happening.

I soon found out what had been happening behind the scenes. Without my knowledge, other people in the lab were moving positions and jobs. On my second day, my new manager asked if I wanted a 32-hour position, and a year later, I was back to the full-time hours we needed. I'm glad we set our sights on what was unseen.

My current job gives us the ability to follow the vision God has given us. Had I waited for it to look the way I envisioned, we might have missed it. We all know life brings new challenges. The challenges are harder to handle when there is no vision. When life is self-centered, every difficulty is overwhelming. I believe this is because the troubles and chaos of life need a reference point, a control group. They need a place to be put in perspective. And we need this perspective as a reminder that life isn't just about us.

The mission has to be greater than you.

Is your current mission bigger than you and your family?
How do you pursue something "bigger"?

Are you capable? Yes. Every person has unique thoughts, abilities, and skills to offer. Our biggest hurdle is comparison. We compare ourselves to every lie that is out there and rarely compare ourselves to the truth.

I've often thought things like:

- If these line up, we can do it.

- If this comes through, I'll be able to make that happen.

- That's never going to happen; I don't see that ever coming together for me.

- It's just not in the cards for me.

- What if I put myself out there and share my ideas and thoughts, and I end up looking like an idiot because I've never done this before?

- I'm not as good of a speaker as she is, and it'll probably be stupid, and no one will listen. So, I'm just gonna binge *The Office Season 5* and disconnect from a mission because it feels too risky.

You are capable; you have value to bring.

Maybe you're asking, how do I find something bigger than me? To find something bigger than us, we have to stop wandering through life and get a vision. I can't stress enough how an opportunity will come when you line up a purpose for what you want to do. When you have a clear vision of where you are going, you can also partner better with someone else's dream or mission.

Kate and I were on the board for a conference in our area. This event aligned with our family vision, which gave us the clarity to say "yes" to it and the compass to navigate our responsibility to the board. It was not my dream, but because we owned our "yes," the conference vision and mission became ours.

What does "bigger than you" mean? I don't know, but it sounds cool. To me, it means the mission I'm a part of is not about me; I'm about it. I know it can happen without me, but I also know I have some resources to push it forward. I have to do it with purpose and on purpose. Our kids and family can't be our end mission; they need to be a part of one. Bear will know he isn't the center of our world. Yes, he was born to be great, and the world needs him to be great, but the reason for greatness isn't selfish. He has value to bring to the mission our family is invested in.

Something more significant than you keeps you from being selfish. A mission challenges you, intimidates you, and pulls the greatness out of you. It will lead you to take a chance. I came across this poem and have had it stored on my phone for more than ten years. I periodically read it to remind myself that I don't want to wander aimlessly, to be compromised by situations or live selfishly. I want to be ready with a go-bag and head into whatever God calls my family and me.

"George Grey"

I have studied many times
The marble which was chiseled for me—
A boat with a furled sail at rest in a harbor.
In truth it pictures not my destination
But my life.
For love was offered me and I shrank from its disillusionment;
Sorrow knocked at my door, but I was afraid;
Ambition called to me, but I dreaded the chances.
Yet all the while I hungered for meaning in my life.
And now I know that we must lift the sail
And catch the winds of destiny
Wherever they drive the boat.
To put meaning in one's life may end in madness,
But life without meaning is the torture
Of restlessness and vague desire—
It is a boat longing for the sea and yet afraid.
(Masters)

My mom spent three months traveling to different cities and mountain villages. She walked, traveled on horseback, and rode buses. She went into homes by simply knocking on the front doors. She spoke in several churches and schools. She gave away 256 Bibles and led 1,650 people to Jesus by the time she came home. My dad spent three months supporting his wife and family spiritually, emotionally, and physically. He helped with homework, made a birthday cake, and got three kids to school on time. They didn't complain to friends about the situation. Instead, they took responsibility for the mission entrusted to them. Mom and Dad lifted the sails to catch the winds of the destiny God had for them. They went for it and did it.

Get a vision. Find a mission. Take a risk.

I LOVE TO CREATE,
WRITE, AND HAVE
A BASKET OF FRUIT
TO SHARE. THESE
TRUTHS ARE YELLING
INTO MY LIFE, AND
MAYBE THEY CAN BE
A CATALYST FOR YOU
AND YOUR FAMILY.
I WANT THEM TO
INSPIRE YOU TO DIG
IN FOR YOURSELF
AND TO LIVE IN FAITH
BETWEEN SUNDAYS.

CHAPTER SIX
Just Jesus

HAVE COUNTLESS MEMORIES OF THE SAME SITUATION. It's like there was a glitch in my Matrix that happened multiple days a week—one person living a deja vu moment. Outfits, hairstyles, and furniture may have changed, but the experience was constant. I would wake up in the morning and roam out to the living room to find Mom, sitting on the corner cushion of the couch with black coffee reading her red Amplified Bible. Her Bible was worn but well kept. She would have a handmade afghan draped over her legs. I have no idea which books or chapters she was reading, but it seemed like she was on to something good.

Sometimes she would read it to me out loud if I sat next to her. And although I can't recall the words, I can remember the coffee breath. Now, as a drinker of the morning pick-me-up myself, I realize coffee breath comes with the territory. I'm amazed that it can smell so good as fresh grounds in the bag, but it leaves a lot to be desired as warm breath from a mouth. That sounds a bit gross, but coming from my mom, it didn't bother me as a kid. Sometimes she would be praying, and my sisters and I would interrupt her study time for breakfast. She would have to break scrub and leave her spiritual heart surgery for us, and she would.

I also remember Dad in the evenings. At the end of my day, he was reading his Dake's Study Bible in the recliner. He would be telling us to go to bed, scribbling in his spiral notebook. He taught Sunday school at church and would prepare his lesson throughout the week. My mind can still put together images of his cursive writing in the Bible's margins. And just like the memory of my mom, it's the same with my dad. Their hunger for God's Word was constant.

Bear has similar memories, at least with Kate. One time, when Bear was about five, I put his Spider-Man hat on and said, "Look I'm Bear, I wear a Spider-man hat." He thought it was hilarious. So, Bear grabbed Kate's Bible and water bottle and said, "Look, I'm Mommy. I drink water and read my Bible." I felt all warm and fuzzy on my insides as memories flooded me back to my childhood. Kate even drinks coffee during her quiet time and sits on the corner cushion with her Bible and journal.

I need to get a better setup. I do the majority of my Bible reading and notes on my phone and iPad. Bear probably thinks I'm wasting my life on electronics. And he has claimed the iPad for himself, so my study time usually ends with a fight between my son and me over whose turn it is to use it. If Bear ever writes a book like this, it'll just say my dad just texted and scrolled his Insta all the time while Mom read the Bible and sought the Lord's face.

By watching my parents, I learned

First, it's best to talk less and listen more.

Second, we only need one book.

Third, we each need to study according to our own design.

It's best to talk less and listen more.

When you're in a conversation, are you waiting to say your point, or are you listening to what's being said?

I tuned into a podcast a while back about leadership. The host, Craig Groeschel, talked about the need for a mentor, someone who knows more about life than you. He said something I could relate to. He said, "I don't recommend going up to someone you admire and asking them to be your mentor. It isn't a comfortable position to put someone in" (Leadership Podcast). I've done this, and it wasn't successful; it was awkward. My potential Mr. Miyagi was taken off guard when I said, "I think God wants you to mentor me."

He responded politely, "Um, okay." I was all in too. I found this guy at church who was nothing like me, didn't know anything about me, and wasn't ready for my boldness. I had no idea what I wanted from a mentor or even needed. So, I approached the idea of being mentored, thinking he'd teach me something profound that applied to my life. But I didn't have any sincere questions to ask. The first time we met was the Christian parallel to the scene in *The Karate Kid* when Daniel Larouso met Mr. Miyagi and asked him to fix the leaking faucet. I was certain he was my guy. We got together four times, but never caught flies with chopsticks, and I never received my lotus flower headband.

I like Craig's recommendation better than my method. He suggests asking someone you admire to coffee or out to lunch. Then ask them a couple of specific questions and listen. It will give purpose and direction to the meeting. Don't keep talking; listen to what they say—this hit home for me with how I relate to God.

I connected what I heard on the podcast to these Scriptures:

> I seek you with all my heart; do not let me stray from
> your commands. I have hidden your word in my heart

that I might not sin against you. Praise be to you, Lord; teach me your decrees. With my lips I recount all the laws that come from your mouth. I rejoice in following your statutes as one rejoices in great riches. I meditate on your precepts and consider your ways. I delight in your decrees; I will not neglect your word. (Psalm 119:10-17 NIV)

I have learned to first seek out a word with my heart. Then, I hide that word in my heart. Finally, I meditate on it and consider all its ways. What a practical guide for spending time with Him.

So how do I apply this with Jesus? I have a list of notes in my phone with those random thoughts that seem to drop in my mind: ideas, questions, something said to me or bothering me, something I want to cultivate in me, or something I want to weed out, and verses from the Bible that I love. In the one on One, I'll choose a topic and jump in. I'll compile verses and listen for God's voice. I reread the verses a few times in several different versions and mull over the vocabulary, surrounding text, and other notes complimenting the topic. Then I soak it in like a lizard in the Mexico sun. I meditate on what I read and consider how to apply it. Then I like to share what I've learned.

But I didn't always love to learn. When I was younger, I wasn't fond of reading, and I was not good at reading aloud. My palms would get clammy, and my forehead would bead up with sweat when I had to read to the class. My teacher went down each row, every student reading the next consecutive paragraph from the textbook. I would count how many kids were in front of me and match the paragraph sections to know which one was mine. Then, I'd silently rehearse the words ten times before it was my turn. I would have no idea what anyone else was reading because I was consumed with what I needed to say. I lived in the panic of the moment, hoping there would be a fire drill. I'd quietly plead my case, "Please, God, let this building burn down before I have to read these twenty-three words out loud."

My point is, if you're so concerned about what you're saying to God or how you're going to say it, you may miss out on what He's speaking to you. As a kid in that class, the entire page contents were being read directly to me, but I didn't hear any of it. I was so anxious about my paragraph and how I relayed it that I didn't comprehend my reading or how it fit the bigger picture. Perhaps God's been speaking into your conversation, but you've been so focused on your twenty-three words you've missed what He's been saying the whole time. If my paragraph is a life experience I'd like to share with God, He has an entire Book of revelation to share with me. Sometimes, the importance of listening in prayer can be overshadowed by talking. He wants to hear what's on our hearts, and He wants to share what's in His. It's a chance to learn from His Word, to learn from His Spirit, and to sit at the Master's feet and listen.

Not sure where to start? Try beginning your time with a question, an idea, or a thought. Then, get into it, searching your Bible for answers, confirmation, and fresh insight. Listen to God, more so than you would Mr. Miyagi. When you find something, hold on to it. Then meditate on it before moving on to something else, giving the Word time to settle into your spirit.

We only need one book.

Is the Bible your central focus when you have time with Jesus?

God's Word and Jesus Christ are one and the same, as explained in John 1:1-5:

"In the beginning [before all time] was the Word (Christ), and the Word was with God, and the Word was God Himself. He was [continually existing] in the beginning [co-eternally] with God. All things were made and came into existence through Him; and without Him not even one thing was made that has come into being" (Amplified Bible). The Word of God, the Christ. I love how this verse says all things were made and came into existence through Him. All learning stems from Jesus. But I have come to love learning from others. I enjoy hearing their views and opinions, even if they're opposed to my own. I read books, listen to podcasts, and watch videos about things I will probably never do, like street fighting or off-grid living (you can imagine how ADD affects YouTube scrolling). When it comes to God and faith, learning is limitless. While others can help us understand and connect with God, books and sermons are no replacement for the Word of God. We can't forget about His direct Word to us because we listen to others tell us about their experience with Him. As God often does, He illustrated this point to me during yard work.

I was cleaning grass and weeds out from around my hostas. Kate and I are not very passionate about plants, so the vegetation had gotten out of hand. One weed, in particular, was extra annoying. The thing looked substantial and covered a lot of ground. But, once I started gathering the little shoots and branches, I found one little superficial root holding it all together, and it pulled out easily. God showed me that an idea or truth shared by someone else could cover a great deal of surface area in life. It can look robust and well-woven into my lifestyle. But like the giant plant with a little anchor, it can be easily replaced and forgotten. I believe it's the difference between being told what to do versus understanding what to do for yourself.

Amazing things are accomplished without understanding. Ownership of knowledge comes with learning and research. For example, a doctor I work with once explained a dysrhythmia to me and asked, "Do you understand what's happening?"

I replied, "I hear what you're saying, and I can repeat it back to you. But no, I don't understand it." His response was encouraging.

He said, "I'm okay with that as long as you keep learning." He was looking out for me, knowing that if I didn't understand what was happening, I wouldn't be able to see what was coming down the pipe. In the same way, the more understanding we gain for ourselves spiritually, the more we can anticipate what God is doing. We need to keep learning for ourselves instead of continually repeating what the great teachers, leaders, and thinkers of our day are saying. It's like needing a middleman in communion; our intimacy can only go so deep.

Not devoting time to listening and learning for ourselves is the equivalent of harvesting someone else's fruit. A farmer does the work to nurture, cultivate, and grow the fruit. When they share it with me, I walk away with a fresh Honeycrisp apple, and it's good. I love that I get to eat it and benefit from the farmer's knowledge and understanding. I share with someone how good the apple was and tell them they should buy from the same farmer because his fruit trees are life-changing. In the same way, we'll listen to podcasts and watch YouTube videos and share with our friends so they can like, subscribe, and share too. Harvesting someone else's fruit, or revelation, isn't a bad thing. However, if we continually take from other people's trees, we forget how to produce fruit of our own.

Please understand: I have done life-changing devotional Bible studies myself. But they change my course because I confirm what I hear and what I read with Scripture and apply it to my life. I've begun letting outside studies compliment or lead me into my gardening session with God instead of them being my primary source of food.

So, why would I write this book if I am directing you back to the one best source? This book has been profound for Kate and me. I love to create, write, and have a basket of fruit to share. These truths are yelling into my life, and maybe they can be a catalyst for you and your family. I want them to inspire you to dig in for yourself and to live in faith between Sundays. I am the person who will benefit most from writing these words. They are more real to me than to you, not because it's mine, in a possessive sense, but because I have been digging into each topic. I have the dirt under my fingernails. I want all of us to break new ground.

It's great to hear someone else's revelation of God, but you will never be the same when you hear God's revelation for you directly from the Word. The information becomes alive. I came across this great story recently and thought this would be an appropriate place to share it.

On September 11, 1918, Sgt. David Ker, a Columbia University student who had dropped out of college to fight in World War I, sent a letter to his mother the day before the attack on Saint-Mihiel in France. While some troops consider it bad luck to write an "in case I die" letter, Ker wanted his mother, sister, and fiancée to keep their spirits up, no matter the outcome.

In the letter, he wrote about all the Americans going out to fight together and not being afraid to die. He wrote to his mom to ensure his sister would be taken care of and that his belongings would be given to his fiancée. It was an amazing letter. The Americans broke through the German lines but suffered 7,000 casualties in the three-day offensive. Twenty-year-old David Ker was among the dead. It sounds sobering to have your final thoughts and directions about what you want written down like Sgt. David Ker. I've told you about the letter and the outcome, but here is the actual letter:

> Tomorrow, the first totally American drive commences, and it gives me inexpressible joy and pride to know that I shall be present to do my share. Should I go under, therefore, I want you to know that I went without any terror of death, and that my chief worry is the grief my death will bring to those so dear to me. Since having found myself and Mary, there has been much to make life sweet and glorious, but death, while distasteful, is in no way terrible.
>
> I feel wonderfully strong to do my share well, and, for my sake, you must try to drown your sorrow in the pride and satisfaction, the knowledge that I died well in so clean a cause, as is ours, should bring you. Remember how proud I have always been of your superb pluck, keep Elizabeth's future in mind, and don't permit my death to bow your head. My personal belongings will all be sent to you. Your good taste will tell you which to send to Mary. May

God bless and keep you, dear heart, and be kind to little Elizabeth, and those others I love so well.

David (Carroll).

That letter hits differently than my description. Could you feel the difference between my second-hand account and your first-hand reading of the letter? The personalization and raw emotion are different, and we read it with a tone and voice that speaks to us. We can transfer this understanding to learning about God. Reading His Word for yourself is an experience no one can recreate.

Dig into the One Book, get your hands dirty, and find the revelation God has for you. And remember, comparison kills vulnerability. So don't compare your garden, your personal time with God, to mine or anyone else's.

We each need to study according to our own design._

Have you attempted to model your connection with God after someone else's?

At the end of last year, when Kate and I were aligning our vision and goals, I purposefully took time on my days off to pursue God. But honestly, I was hit-and-miss. I would see Kate doing it so naturally, but I would struggle to find the time, keep the time, and pay attention during the time. I have a solid memory of sitting down to pray, and during my prayer, my mind strayed to a documentary about "the tree man" in Indonesia. Look it up some time, and it will blow your mind. I wasn't able to recover from my brain drift that morning. I apologized to God and said, "I'll try again later." Kate had what seemed like stacks of journals lying around holding pro-

found life dissections with God. And there I was, wondering if
tree man syndrome was contagious.

Honestly, I was irritated. I would watch Kate read, journal,
and share what she was learning. Then, as if I was a sixth grad-
er mocking my sister, I'd think, "Wow, that's soooo cooooool
for you. I love that for you. Neat." Then I'd go read random
chapters and squeeze together the drop of a feeling that "I did
it too." Finally, I'd move on with my lie that I was getting the
same quality fruit, although my study time looked different.
But I wasn't.

I embraced many rationalizations. I'm not like Kate. My
mind works differently. I don't have the luxury of being home
and choosing how I fill my schedule. I'm booked between a
full-time job that requires overtime, home responsibilities,
church, and volunteering, plus Bible study and family events.
So, I talk to God throughout the day. I pray on my ride to work
and read my Bible when I have time. Plus, my ADD doesn't
let me study as she does. I saw a commercial about ADD meds
once, and I could completely relate. The commercial showed
someone's mind, like TV channels changing nonstop. I can be
doing a project at home, and I will start a new one in the middle of doing it. This was true for my Bible time as well, and it's
why I have bonus rounds in this book.

But believing that my processor is broken because of ADD
will lead me to believe I am defective. I know that isn't true.
By now, we know that's not what He says about who I am. I
needed to connect with God; it was time to go to a deeper level. I realized God was asking more of me. One night at church
Bible study, I led a men's small group. I don't know what the
topic was about, but it stirred in me the thought, "God wants

me to burn hotter. To go deeper." I felt like God was saying, "We have been maintaining our relationship, and now it's time to know more of each other."

I was partially offended by the term "maintaining." It sounded like we were just getting by, like casual acquaintances. But it was more like our relationship was burning at 1,000 degrees, and He wanted to crank it up to 1,500. He was showing me there's more of Him to know. As I spilled my guts, like people do in small groups, half of the guys didn't know what to think. But I had to get this thought out of my head. I had to get eyes on it.

I needed to do a couple things before I could burn hotter. First, eliminate excuses. I've learned that distraction while focusing will always be present, no matter what level of a deficit your attention has disordered. Focused time with God can't happen while I'm doing other activities. My schedule and brain function are embarrassing excuses to not meet up with God, intentionally.

I've also realized there are many areas where I focus well. At work, I can be easily sidetracked. But relaxing my focus when someone is actively dying would be a sig-

> One day, I thought I'd help out around the house. I picked up Legos on the floor before vacuuming when I spotted some popcorn kernels. I paused with the Legos to throw the seeds away. I noticed the curtains were unevenly closed on my way to the trash, so I adjusted all three sets. Then, I regrouped the kernels. The garbage was full, so I emptied it, noticing leaves on the porch on my way to the trash can. I meandered into the garage to grab the leaf blower and took care of those pesky tree droppings. I blew off the porch, then went back inside to vacuum when I realized I needed to leave for an appointment. The vacuuming would have to wait. Distractions happen.

nificant problem for both parties involved. So, I concentrate on the task at hand, and I'm pretty good at it. In our downtime at the ole' job site, I go over the necessary equipment to keep my mind sharp and appreciate learning from my coworkers. This is true at home as well. Yes, my thoughts drift with the breeze, but I have several focused, intentional conversations with my wife, friends, and strangers every day. I can direct my attention. And this translates to my relationship with God. I need to step past the valued mentor, job, and people in my life to connect with Him. I have removed the lie that I don't have the attention span to have "one-on-One" time with God.

After eliminating excuses, I needed to stop comparing. Yes, Kate and I think differently, but she's not more able to connect with God than I am. Unfortunately, the initial thought led me into a progress-stunting lie. In truth, we are all different. We learn differently, understand differently, teach differently, and focus differently. But we all grow in intimacy and friendship the same way— by talking and listening with purposeful time together. And if I wanted to burn hotter, I needed to unhitch my wagon from comparison and couple with my design.

Notice what the writer of this psalm asks of God: "Be good to your servant while I live, that I may obey your word. Open my eyes that I may see wonderful things in your law. I am a stranger on earth; do not hide your commands from me" (Psalm 119:17-19 NIV). The writer asks God to open his eyes to see the wonderful things in His law. In His Word. He's looking to God's revelation for him, not another person's revelation of God.

What then does it mean to study by design? I can see a parallel between Kate's design and my mom's. Both can read and write, with no other agenda. They just do it to know God more. Kate is like a data miner. She loves knowledge and has a deep understanding of who He is to her.

My design parallels my dad's. He would study for himself so he could share and give to others. I need an outlet. Whether it's talking to a friend or my wife, creating a podcast, or writing a book. By design, I like to share thoughts and ideas. When I couple my design to God, spending time in the Bible becomes natural to me. Writing a book of stories or a lecture series, as weird as it is to some of you, seems perfectly logical to me. I enjoy building things: farmhouse tables, songs, conferences. I've found that I give more of myself to God when I study by creating something. It helps me understand. And it helps me look for the pieces I need to accomplish it.

When I spoke these ideas initially as a lecture series at a local coffee shop, I would get nervous that it wouldn't make any sense. But once I started speaking, I no longer felt intimidated because I could see the fruit I was sharing. I wanted to scream, "LOOK WHAT I CREATED!!!!" like Tom Hanks in *Cast Away* when he makes fire.

Kate will confirm that a phrase I use a lot is, "You've got to see this." I want you to experience what I'm experiencing. I have made Kate come and look at mole tunnels in our yard while I explain what I know, how I know it, and what I think about it. She needs to know what I think about the moles and the best solution to killing these little creatures the Lord created. That has to be annoying a little, but not to Kate. She can't get enough of me.

So, when I read the Bible, I often build something to show someone. I will put my thoughts about what I read into a paragraph to see my learning grow into understanding. Then I look at what I found, and say to Kate, "You have to see this."

Creative-driven studying works for me. Take time to think about what works for you. Understand how you learn and how you connect with God between Sundays. Look at what inspires physical community with people and find the correlation spiritually with God. Then, when you personalize your time with God, get into your Bible, and listen more. Maybe like Mom and Dad, grab your afghan, snoogy, or fleece tie blanket and put on some coffee. Or like Kate, journal and mine His Word. You might feel the urge to create what He is showing to then share with someone. However, God designed you, tap into that and get your hands dirty. Show up consistently to hear His voice and His revelation for you.

WHAT WE ARE DOING BETWEEN SUNDAYS IS WHERE IT MATTERS. LIVE YOUR FAITH WITH PURPOSE.

Conclusion

M Y MOM LIKES TO USE THE WORD "RICH" to describe a decadent dessert. All you need is a small portion to feel like you've indulged. She uses the same phrase to describe a hug or kiss from her family. "Que rico," she says after a bear hug from her kids, grandkids, or great-grandkids. "Where your treasure is there your heart will be," the Bible tells us. I know my parent's treasure is in Jesus and their family. There was a richness in my childhood that had nothing to do with money or material things. Is your life decadent, sweet, and indulging for those around you? Is there a richness beyond material things?

Thinking back to my childhood memories, Kate and I were face to face with these questions. Although my parents seemed to live out the six topics in this book organically, I only sporadically implemented them with my family.

When we started having communion, we felt something shifting inside of us. It's easy to feel like you're forcing it but experiencing Jesus at home became more natural the more purposeful we became. Over time, many areas we've discussed have become second nature, authentic, and customized for our family. We hope that generations of Thompsons to come will invite Jesus into their homes to experience the wealth of knowing Him.

As we come to the final section, I hope you've found a place to start. I hope this book propels you into more time with Jesus. Don't over-strategize and fail to take action. Take communion with your friends and family often. Don't wait for the church service to lead you. Build relationships with people around you who catapult you forward towards Him. Find community to help you pull specks from your eyes. Be vulnerable. Show the kindness of Christ without a meter. Freely give the love that was given to you. Discover your identity from Him. You were born to be great, the world needs you to be great, God designed you to be great. Collaborate with something bigger than you. Get a vision of where you are going, find a mission to be a part of, and take the risk. Yesterday is gone, and tomorrow may never come. What we are doing between Sundays is where it matters. Live your faith with purpose. Live richly, my friends.

Works Cited

Carroll, Andrew. "Final Letters from Fallen Warriors." *AARP Bulletin.* https://www.aarp.org/home-family/friends-family/info-2014/soldiers-last-letter-home.html

Cron, Ian Morgan. "A Thirst for Redemption featuring Scott Harrison." *Typology Podcast,* season 2, episode 10. https://podcasts.apple.com/us/podcast/courage-in-vulnerability-feat-chris-cruz-enneagram-8/id1254061093?i=1000423911136

Cunnington, Havilah. *Eat Pray Hustle.* eBook. Havilahcunnington.com, 2015.

Groeschel, Craig. "Creating a Value-Driven Culture, Part 1." *Leadership Podcast,* episode 5, March 3, 2016.

Keller, Timothy. *The Reason for God.* London: Penguin Books, 2015.

Masters, Edgar Lee. 1915. http://poets.org/poem/george-gray.

A note from the authors

W<small>E ARE</small> N<small>ATE AND</small> K<small>ATE</small> T<small>HOMPSON</small> and *Between Sundays* is our first book. Thank you for opening it up and letting your mind wander into the words and stories that have been so fun to write. We love pursuing Jesus and being creative with whatever he entrusts to us. We believe that God is always willing to do a new thing and wants everyone of us to join Him! Thank you so much for purchasing this book. We hope you enjoyed reading it as much as we enjoyed making it.

When not working or writing, Nate can be found on YouTube or iTunes as the co-host of the Full Send Living Podcast.

We'd love to connect with you even further through Instagram too: @1natethompson

If you'd like to share how *Between Sundays* has made an impact on your life or have questions for us, send us an e-mail: nethomp@rocketmail.com

Thanks for sharing life with us,

Nate and Kate Thompson

Made in the USA
Middletown, DE
16 June 2022